THE CAMBRIDGE BIBLE COMMENTARY

NEW ENGLISH BIBLE

GENERAL EDITORS

P. R. ACKROYD, A. R. C. LEANEY, J. W. PACKER

OLD TESTAMENT ILLUSTRATIONS

OLD TESTAMENT ILLUSTRATIONS

Photographs, maps and diagrams
compiled and introduced by

CLIFFORD M. JONES

University of Leeds Institute of Education

CAMBRIDGE
AT THE UNIVERSITY PRESS
1971

Published by the Syndics of the Cambridge University Press
Bentley House, 200 Euston Road, London N.W.1
American Branch: 32 East 57th Street, New York, N.Y.10022

© Cambridge University Press 1971

Library of Congress Catalogue Card Number: 76–142131

ISBN: 0 521 08007 X

Printed in Great Britain
by Jarrold & Sons Ltd, Norwich

GENERAL EDITORS' PREFACE

The aim of this series is to provide commentaries and other books about the Bible, based on the text of the New English Bible, and in these various volumes to make available to the general reader the results of modern scholarship. Teachers and young people have been especially kept in mind. The commentators have been asked to assume no specialized theological knowledge, and no knowledge of Greek or Hebrew. Bare references to other literature and multiple references to other parts of the Bible have been avoided. Actual quotations have been given as often as possible.

This volume is designed to provide, in the form of maps, diagrams and photographs, information which will supplement the commentaries, giving in some detail, and in graphic form, material which can at best be briefly alluded to in that series. It is linked by its content with two other volumes, (1) *Understanding the Old Testament*, which sets out to provide the larger historical and archaeological background, to say something about the life and thought of the people of the Old Testament, and to try to answer the question 'Why should we study the Old Testament?' (2) *The Making of the Old Testament*, which is concerned with the formation of the books of the Old Testament and Apocrypha in the context of the ancient near eastern world, and with the ways in which these books have come down to us in the life of the Jewish and Christian communities. These three volumes have been designed to provide material helpful to the understanding of the individual books and their commentaries, but can be used quite independently of them. The success of similar volumes in the New Testament series encourages the belief that these will be found equally valuable to a wide range of readers.

P.R.A.
A.R.C.L.
J.W.P.

AUTHOR'S NOTE

My sincere thanks are freely offered to the following for their valuable assistance in the production of this book: the General Editors of *The Cambridge Bible Commentary* for their many suggestions for the improvement of the manuscript; the editorial staff of the Cambridge University Press for their help with the technical details of production; the Reverend H. St J. Hart, Queens' College, Cambridge, for the photographs of coins (**134–54**) and the information about them; and Mr D. R. Ap-Thomas, University College of North Wales, Bangor, for advice on the topography of Jerusalem (**56**).   C.M.J.

CONTENTS

ACKNOWLEDGEMENTS

The author and publishers are grateful to the following for permission to reproduce photographs.

45. The late Professor F. S. Bodenheimer; **163–7.** The British and Foreign Bible Society; **103, 112, 123, 126, 160, 176, 194.** The Bible Lands Society (The Old Kiln, Hazlemere, High Wycombe, Bucks.); **9, 10, 17, 19, 23, 24, 33, 68, 71, 72, 77, 80, 81, 85, 89, 92, 130, 132, 158, 159, 162.** The British Museum; **99.** The Brooklyn Museum; **97, 98.** Professor George G. Cameron, *The American School of Oriental Research and the University of Michigan*; **7, 8, 34, 35, 38, 58, 67, 86, 109, 118, 119, 129, 131, 170, 174.** J. Allan Cash; **27.** Maurice Chuzeville, Vanves, France; **100.** Clarendon Press: *New Clarendon Bible: Israel under Mesopotamia and Persia*, P. R. Ackroyd, 1970; **134–54.** The Reverend H. St J. Hart; **124, 125.** Israel Department of Antiquities and Museums; **106–8, 110, 113, 169.** A. F. Kersting; **195.** Leeds City Art Galleries; **12, 13, 20, 25, 28, 32, 36, 37, 39–41, 60, 70, 73–6, 82–4, 87, 91, 94–6, 175, 197, 200.** The Mansell Collection; **57.** The Matson Photo Service; **22.** Ministry of Defence (Air Force Department), Crown copyright reserved; **173.** Le Musée du Louvre; **5, 21, 47, 62, 63, 122, 172.** Oriental Institute, University of Chicago; **50.** Oxford University Press (Illustration by Carel Weight from *The Oxford Illustrated Old Testament*, vol. 2 The Historical Books – Joshua to Esther); **182.** The Press Association; **29, 42, 48, 49, 55, 69, 93, 102, 114–17, 120, 121, 127, 128, 183, 186, 191–3, 196, 199, 201.** Radio Times Hulton Picture Library; **133.** Rijksmuseum van Oudheden, Leiden; **177, 179.** Southeastern Films, Atlanta; **184, 189, 190, 190, 198.** University of London, The Warburg Institute; **30, 43, 44, 46, 51, 61, 105, 111, 156, 157, 161, 168, 171, 185, 187, 188.** Willem Van de Poll; **78, 79, 90.** The Wellcome Trust.

ABOUT THIS BOOK

The Bible is often said to be a best seller, and statistics confirm the truth of the statement; but it cannot safely be assumed that all those who buy the Bible also read it regularly or with understanding. Many who begin to study the Bible find its language so technical and its ancient eastern background so unfamiliar that they are unable to derive from it either enjoyment or profit, and they quickly give up the attempt to make sense of it and eventually cease to read it.

The Old Testament in particular suffers in this respect. More daunting in size, much more diverse in content and style, and much more remote from us in time than the New Testament, it is for many, both literally and metaphorically, a closed book. If, as Christians claim, the Bible is the Word of God, this neglect of it is particularly serious. Can anything be done to stimulate greater interest in the Old Testament and to make it more comprehensible to those who read it? This volume has been compiled in the belief that it can. Old Testament topics are illustrated by means of photographs, maps and plans, charts and diagrams, and brief explanatory comments accompany the illustrations. In this way it is hoped that light will be thrown on the background of the Old Testament and that deeper understanding of the history and religion of Israel and her neighbours will result.

It cannot be claimed that the Apocrypha and the Old Testament are completely and evenly covered in this book, for the simple reason that not all parts of the Bible are equally suitable for illustration by means of the graphic arts. The content of the book has therefore been partly determined by the illustrations that are available. This collection of illustrations is intended as a companion to the Old Testament volumes of *The Cambridge Bible Commentary*, and the serious student will fill the obvious gaps in this book by studying it side by side with the commentaries.

A large number of the photographs are of archaeological remains, and in studying them it is particularly important to remember what biblical archaeology is, and what it is not; what it claims to do, and what it does not claim to do. Chapter 2 should therefore be carefully read, so that unwarranted conclusions are not drawn from the considerable number of illustrations of archaeological subjects.

Postage stamps issued by countries in the Near East frequently depict Old Testament subjects, but for technical reasons it has not been possible to reproduce photographs of any of them here. Stamp-collectors reading this book may find this an interesting and instructive aspect of their hobby, and they will be able to obtain lists from the usual agents. Mr M. H. Bale, 41 High Street, Ilfracombe, England, is a recognized specialist in this field.

Although this collection of illustrations has been compiled with *The Cambridge Bible Commentary* specially in mind, it can equally well be used with another standard commentary on the Old Testament, or indeed without resort to any commentary. The indexes have been prepared with special care, so that if they are consulted and the references are followed up, it will often be the case that light will be thrown on the subject being studied, and the reader will be helped to reach a better understanding of a difficult Bible passage or to gain a visual impression of a biblical incident, an Old Testament location, or a religious object.

The Background of the
Old Testament

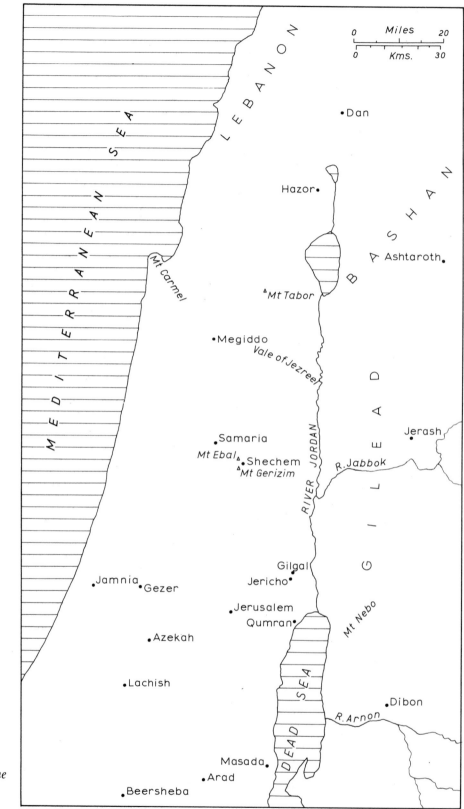

1 *Palestine*

1 GEOGRAPHICAL

Palestine (map **I**) is a rectangle of land about 240 kilometres (150 miles) long and about 120 kilometres (75 miles) wide, bounded on the west by the Mediterranean Sea and on the east and south by desert and hill country. Diagram **2** gives a general impression of the heights and depths in an east–west cross-section of this 'land of mountains and valleys' (Deut. 11: 11). At different latitudes these features vary, of course, but it is not too far from the truth to say that strips of SEA – PLAIN – HILL – VALLEY – TABLELAND run north–south for most of the length of Palestine. There are, however, some important breaks in the ranges of hills to the east and west of the Jordan Valley: to the east, the gorges formed by the rivers Jabbok and Arnon, and to the west, the Vale of Jezreel (map **I**).

    The vertical and horizontal scales in the diagram are widely different. If the vertical scale agreed with the horizontal scale, the heights and depths would scarcely be visible. One effect of this scale difference is to exaggerate enormously the hill slopes, and this must be taken into account when consulting the diagram.

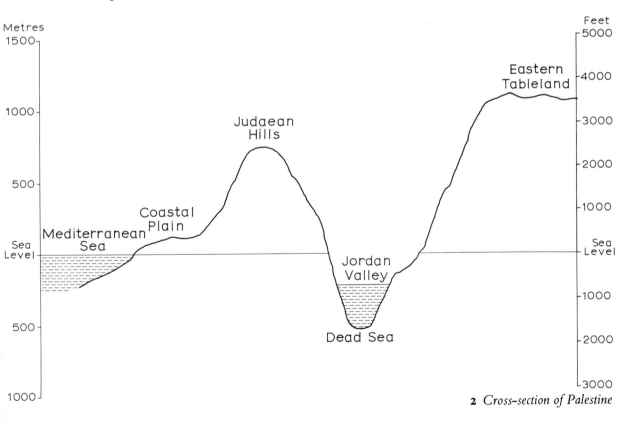

2 *Cross-section of Palestine*

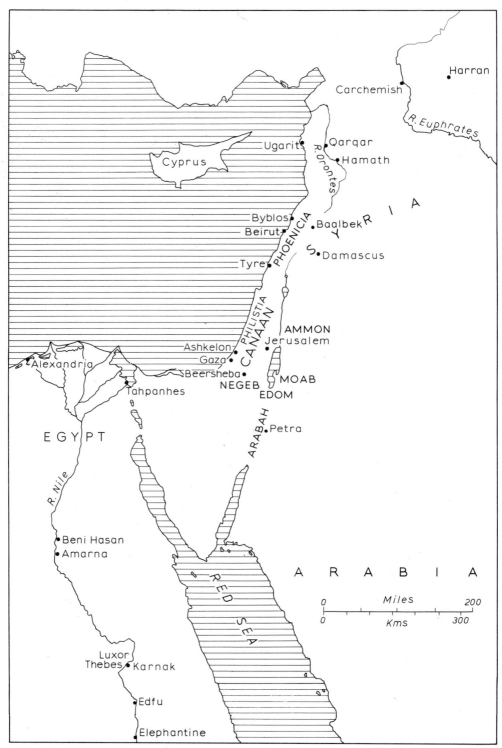

3 *Lands of the Old Testament*

Palestine is remarkably situated in a central position in the Near East; with Syria, Assyria, Babylon and Persia to the north and east, and Egypt, Greece and Rome to the south and west. Maps **3** and **4** show the position of Palestine with respect to the lands that played a prominent part in the history of the period covered by the Old Testament.

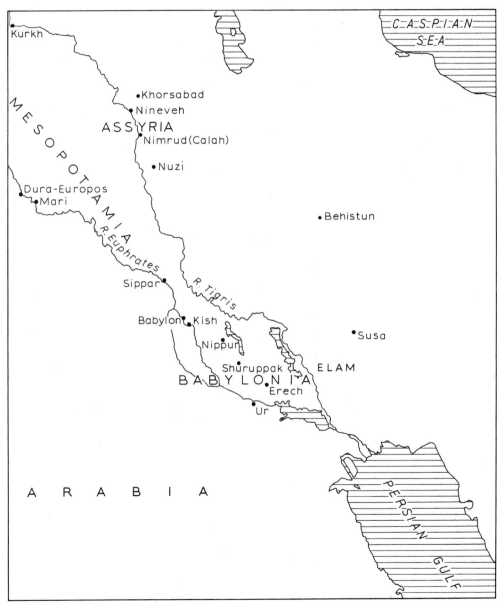

4 *Lands of the Old Testament*

2 ARCHAEOLOGICAL

BIBLICAL ARCHAEOLOGY

The word 'archaeology' is derived from two Greek words, the first of which, *arche*, means 'beginning' and the second of which, *logia*, means 'a branch of knowledge'. By derivation, therefore, archaeology is the branch of knowledge that deals with beginnings or origins; and archaeologists are people who try to reach back in time to discover the original records of civilizations, communities, buildings, documents, works of art, or other objects of human interest. It is not always possible to reach back so far, however, and it is better to define archaeology in more realistic terms and to say that it is the study of the remains that people of earlier ages have left behind. Biblical archaeology is a special branch of the subject, concerned only with the remains of those people of earlier ages who are associated with the Bible.

Contrary to popular opinion, archaeology is not treasure-hunting, and the aim of biblical archaeology is not to prove the truth of the Bible. Before the subject was properly understood, explorers who had the necessary time and money visited those parts of the world where the remains of ancient civilizations were to be found, and employed native workmen to dig for archaeological treasure. The results of their random digging and their tomb-plundering are exhibited in the museums of the world. Such expeditions were often financed by wealthy benefactors who were concerned to demonstrate the literal truth of the Bible, and any discovery that seemed to confirm the accuracy of a text was hailed with delight, and any discovery that did not was often quietly ignored. A second glance at the previous paragraph will show how far such people were from achieving the real object of archaeology.

Biblical archaeology, then, does not set out to show that the Bible is true, but it does contribute enormously to our understanding of the Bible, and to our knowledge of the background against which it was written. Sometimes it supports the biblical record (for example, the patriarchal period, pp. 30ff.); at other times it does not (for example, the destruction of the walls of Jericho, pp. 55f.). To accept evidence that confirms one's own ideas and to ignore that which does not is unscientific to say the least.

Some of the remains that people of earlier ages have left behind are found above the ground; other remains are found only by digging for them below the ground. Material of the latter kind has sometimes been deliberately deposited underground; for example, in the tombs found in ancient burial places, but more often it is there by an accident of history that must now be described.

EXCAVATING A TELL

Ancient habitations were frequently visited by war, fire, famine, or pestilence, and in such circumstances the inhabitants fled, often in great haste, leaving behind many of their possessions. In course of time the houses and other buildings fell into ruins, and the debris became covered with rain-carried silt brought down from a neighbouring hill, by ash from a nearby volcano, or by wind-blown sand or light soil. If the site was a valuable one a new habitation was built, often several centuries later, on the covered ruins of the earlier one, and this in turn was deserted, covered, and built on again. In some cases the process was repeated many times, resulting in the formation of a mound called a tell (from the Arabic word for a hill). At Megiddo, for example (map **1**), twenty levels of human occupation have been uncovered, the lowest, and therefore the earliest, of them dated soon after 5000 B.C. (**5**). A city tell is distinguished from a natural hill by its comparatively flat top and the peculiar slope of its sides (**78**), and these features are most easily seen nowadays by photography from the air.

Several methods of excavating a tell are possible. Because they all attempt to expose the layers or strata of the mound the operation is known as stratigraphy. The most obvious method is to remove successive layers until the lowest layer is reached, like cutting slices horizontally from a loaf of bread. Slicing a tell, however, is a laborious and expensive operation, and on that account it is very rarely used today. The top four layers of Megiddo were completely removed by this method, but the work was stopped by the outbreak of World War II and it has not since been resumed on such a scale.

As early as 1890, W. Flinders Petrie used a more economical and less laborious technique. He excavated Tell el-Hesi, a mound about 36 metres (118 feet) high, situated about 11 kilometres (7 miles) south-west of Lachish (map **1**), by cutting

5 *Excavation levels at Megiddo*

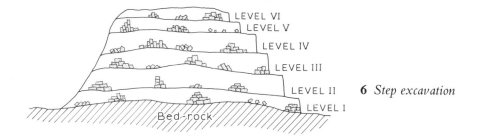

LEVEL VI
LEVEL V
LEVEL IV
LEVEL III
LEVEL II
LEVEL I
Bed-rock

6 *Step excavation*

a series of steps in the side of the hill, each step corresponding to a level of occupation. This diagram (**6**) illustrates the method. Six layers of covered ruins are shown, the earliest of them resting on the bed-rock below which no building can have taken place. The steps that were dug out are seen on the right of the diagram, but it must not be assumed that layers are always as undisturbed as those shown diagrammatically here. In the excavation of a tell the pottery and other objects found in each layer must be kept separately and carefully labelled. Petrie developed a method of distinguishing and dating the pottery he found at Tell el-Hesi and he was thus able to assign a date to each level of occupation.

Another method of stratigraphy is to cut a trench across the top of the tell to the depth of the latest level of occupation, and then to deepen the trench until

7 *Trench excavation at Jericho*

the next level is reached, and to continue the process until bed-rock is reached. Jericho (map **1**) has been partly excavated by this means (**7**). A still more economical method is to dig pits at various points on the tell, exposing levels of

8 *Pit excavation at Jericho*

occupation in a more restricted way than even in the trench method. One such pit can be seen in the foreground of this photograph of the tell at Jericho (**8**). All stratigraphy, whether by the slice, the step, the trench, or the pit method, has the same object: namely, to expose cross-sections of a city or other habitation from its latest to its earliest occupation.

ANCIENT WRITING MATERIALS

The search for buildings and other objects related to the social, religious and cultural life of the people of Bible times is not the only concern of biblical archaeologists. They also hope to find written records that will tell them something of the history, literature and life of earlier ages in the lands of the Bible. Records of this kind are sometimes carved in stone (for example, **34**), or written with a fine brush on bits of broken pottery (for example, **90**); in which case they have survived. At other times the records were written on animal skins, parchment, or papyrus; in which case they are more likely to have perished or become illegible. Many examples of the latter kind have survived only because they were buried in the hot, dry sand of Egypt or some other country with the same kind of climate; or because they were carefully wrapped in damp-proof coverings (for example, **157**).

Ancient scrolls which have been buried in the sand or hidden away in caves or cupboards are dry and brittle when they are discovered many centuries later, and the unrolling of them is a delicate operation requiring enormous patience and very great skill. The animal skins of the Dead Sea scrolls (pp. 139f.) and the papyrus of the Elephantine letters (pp. 99ff.) required this expert treatment to enable these precious documents to be unrolled without damaging the material or spoiling the writing.

OTHER ARCHAEOLOGICAL TECHNIQUES

Excavation is different from nearly every other scientific exercise, in that it cannot be repeated. A laboratory experiment in physics or chemistry can be performed over and over again for purposes of demonstration, but once a layer has been removed from a tell it cannot be replaced exactly as it was when it was originally found, and then removed again to demonstrate the nature of the operation.

9 *Figure of a goat found at Ur*

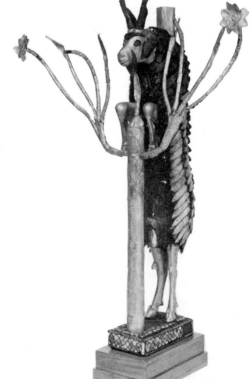

10 *Figure of a goat restored*

Excavation destroys its evidence almost as soon as it is discovered, and it is therefore extremely important that during the digging very careful records should be kept. The position of each find must be carefully noted, drawings must be made, photographs from several different angles, in black and white and in colour, must be taken, and records must be kept of all the relevant circumstances associated with every part of the work. At the end of each day's digging the finds must be cleaned, classified and catalogued.

Some of the objects found may be in need of restoration for exhibition and study purposes, and this may require several months of expert craftsmanship. The first photograph (9) was taken at Ur by C. L. Woolley. It shows an object uncovered but not yet removed from the ground. It is quite flat, having been exposed to great pressure by the weight of soil above it for very many centuries. The next photograph (10) shows the same object after skilful restoration. The head, which was broken in eighteen pieces when it was first discovered, has been repaired, and the crushed body has been modelled to the three-dimensional shape it originally had. This remarkable figure of an animal, representing either a goat caught in a bush or a goat feeding from a tree, was found in the royal cemetery at Ur and it is dated about 2600 B.C. Skilful work of this kind is being patiently carried out in many parts of the world, and our knowledge of ancient civilizations is gradually being built up, not least in those lands associated with the Bible.

Technical applications of modern science are used today to help the archaeologist in his work. It is said that Petrie (see pp. 17f.) handled 50,000 bits of broken pottery to enable him to date the occupation levels at Tell el-Hesi. Nowadays, microphotography and chemical analysis, much more refined and much less laborious methods than Petrie knew, are used to identify and classify pottery. Surveying a site has been greatly simplified by the use of aerial photography. Vertical, oblique, and stereoscopic shots give information almost immediately that might take months to obtain by a ground survey. Infra-red plates and filters cut out haze and make it possible to take photographs of extensive areas from great heights (for example, 43). Ultra-violet photography brings out the writing and makes it readable in a document badly darkened by age, and reveals additions or alterations in the original text of a manuscript.

Science has given archaeologists valuable tools with which to date certain of their finds. A substance containing carbon can be dated by the radio-carbon method. This technique was used to date the linen coverings in which some of the Dead Sea scrolls were wrapped (pp. 139f.). Writing materials made from leather can be dated by a method used in the University of Leeds on fragments of the Dead Sea scrolls. The amount of shrinkage of a shred of leather with rising temperature is determined by its age, and this gives a quick and simple method of dating this kind of document.

Without doubt, the further use of scientific methods of investigation and the application of new techniques to archaeological problems will bring to light new discoveries, and these in turn will lead us to a greater knowledge of the history, customs and beliefs of the people of the Bible, to a better understanding of the text of the Bible, and to a more profound appreciation of the Bible and of its meaning for mankind today. These, whether we achieve them soon or late, are the aims of biblical archaeology.

This time-chart (11) gives in diagrammatic form a summary of the history of the period covered by the Old Testament and the Apocrypha. The chronology of this period presents some difficult problems, and scholars differ in the dates they suggest for some of the events mentioned in it. For example, it is not easy to

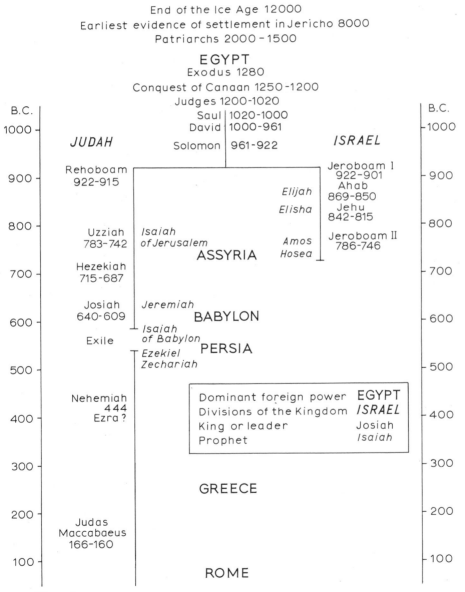

End of the Ice Age 12000
Earliest evidence of settlement in Jericho 8000
Patriarchs 2000-1500

EGYPT
Exodus 1280
Conquest of Canaan 1250-1200
Judges 1200-1020
Saul 1020-1000
David 1000-961
Solomon 961-922

B.C.				B.C.
1000	JUDAH		ISRAEL	1000

Rehoboam 922-915 — Jeroboam I 922-901
Elijah — Ahab 869-850
Elisha — Jehu 842-815
Uzziah 783-742 — Isaiah of Jerusalem — ASSYRIA — Amos Hosea — Jeroboam II 786-746
Hezekiah 715-687
Josiah 640-609 — Jeremiah — BABYLON
Exile — Isaiah of Babylon — PERSIA
Ezekiel Zechariah
Nehemiah 444 — Ezra?

Dominant foreign power EGYPT
Divisions of the Kingdom *ISRAEL*
King or leader Josiah
Prophet *Isaiah*

GREECE

Judas Maccabaeus 166-160

ROME

11 *Time-chart*

decide whether Ezra or Nehemiah returned first from Babylon to Jerusalem after the exile. The date of Nehemiah's return can be established with reasonable certainty (pp. 100f.), but, although it is now generally assumed that Ezra returned to Jerusalem later than Nehemiah, no date can be confidently assigned to Ezra's return.

Only a representative few of the kings and the prophets of the kingdoms of Israel and Judah can be shown on a diagram of this kind, and the standard textbooks on the subject must be consulted for further details.

1. ORIGINS

Creation

The Old Testament opens with 'the story of the making of heaven and earth when they were created' (Gen. 2: 4), and it tells how 'God created man in his own image' (Gen. 1: 27).

12 *The Creation of Man, Michelangelo, Sistine Chapel*

In 1507 Michelangelo (1475–1564), by command of Pope Julius II, began the decoration of the vaulted ceiling of the Sistine Chapel in the Vatican, Rome; a gigantic task which took him five years to complete. *The Creation of Man* (**12**) fills one of the panels in the flat central part of the ceiling. It shows God on the right, supported and surrounded by heavenly beings; and Adam on the left 'in the image of God' (Gen. 1: 27). Eve is held in God's arm and partly hidden behind his body. The New Testament teaches that 'God is spirit' (John 4: 24), but this painting, like the story in Genesis, represents God in the form of a man.

The first eleven chapters of Genesis read like attempts by Hebrew story-tellers to answer some of the questions asked by early man: How was the world made? Where did the first man and woman come from? Why do men and women experience pain? What is the origin of the rainbow? Why do people speak different languages? Questions of this kind were not only asked by Hebrews; people of every race asked them in the early stages of their civilization, and story-tellers in many parts of the world gave similar answers to those found in Genesis 1–11.

In particular, it is known that probably soon after 2000 B.C. Babylonian poets composed poems about the Creation, for copies of them, probably made in the seventh century B.C. were found in the libraries of the kings of Assyria at Nineveh (map 4) during excavations carried out between 1848 and 1876 by A. H. Layard and others. Fragments of some of these tablets found at Nineveh are now in the British Museum (13). The Babylonian story of the Creation on these tablets bears some resemblance to the biblical story, but there are also significant differences in the two accounts. For example, the stories agree about the order in which Creation took place, but they differ profoundly in their views of the Creator.

13 *Creation tablets*

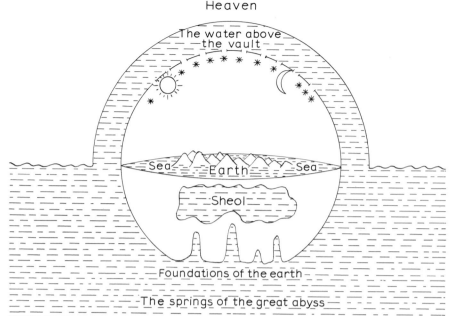

Heaven

The water above the vault

Sea — Earth — Sea

Sheol

Foundations of the earth

The springs of the great abyss

The Old Testament is not a scientific textbook and nowhere does it describe in precise detail the structure of the universe. From scattered verses, which do not always agree, it is possible, however, to represent in diagrammatic form the view of the universe held by the Hebrews in Old Testament times (**14**). 'The foundations of earth' (Psalm 18: 15) support the universe, and stand in 'the springs of the great abyss' (Gen. 7: 11), known elsewhere as 'the deep that lurks below' (Gen. 49: 25). 'The vault of heaven' (Gen. 1: 14), 'spread out . . . like a tent' (Ps. 104: 2), and shining like 'a mirror of cast metal' (Job 37: 18), holds sun, moon and stars, too many to count (Gen. 15: 5). The earth is surrounded by sea, described as 'the water under the vault' (Gen. 1: 7); and Sheol, the abode of the dead, is like 'a great chasm' which 'opens its mouth and swallows them and all that is theirs' (Num. 16: 30). When 'the windows of the sky' (Gen. 7: 11) are opened the water above the vault pours through them, emptying 'the cisterns of heaven' (Job 38: 37), and falls as rain on the earth.

The Lord's throne is in 'the highest heaven' (Deut. 10: 14), the 'heaven of heavens' (Ps. 148: 4); above the earth, above 'the vault of heaven' (Gen. 1: 14), and even higher than the 'waters above the heavens' (Ps. 148: 4).

The Babylonian epic of Creation (p. 25) contains descriptive material from which it is possible to represent in diagrammatic form the view of the universe held by the Babylonians in early times (**15**). The Egyptian picture of the universe (**16**) is probably earlier than either the Babylonian or the Hebrew pictures, but it is not known with certainty if the Hebrew picture is derived from either of the earlier ones.

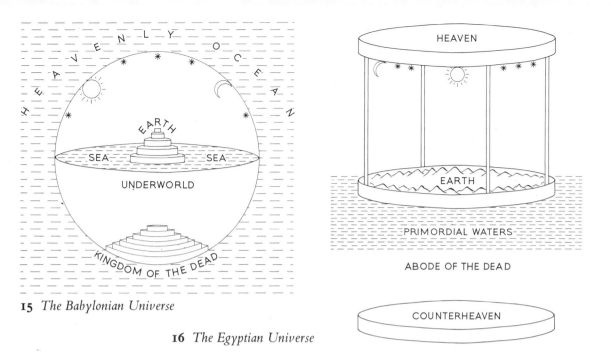

15 *The Babylonian Universe*

16 *The Egyptian Universe*

HEAVEN

EARTH

PRIMORDIAL WATERS

ABODE OF THE DEAD

COUNTERHEAVEN

The flood

Some of the clay tablets found in the libraries at Nineveh (map **4**) have inscribed on them a long poem called the Epic of Gilgamesh. It was evidently a popular poem, for copies of it on clay tablets have been found in several places in the Near and Middle East. It includes a story about a great flood (**17**). The story is written in the form of a myth, but the figure of Gilgamesh may be based on a real king who ruled over Erech (map **4**) in ancient times. Early writers may have told the story of the flood to represent the belief that the human race had suffered an almost universal disaster of some kind in prehistoric times. In addition, however, the Bible story gives pre-scientific explanations of the constancy of the seasons,

17 *Flood tablet*

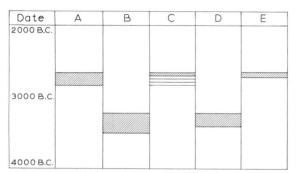

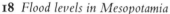

18 *Flood levels in Mesopotamia*

19 *Flood deposit at Ur*

'seedtime and harvest, cold and heat, summer and winter, day and night' (Gen. 8: 22); and of the appearance of 'the bow . . . seen in the cloud' after rain (Gen. 9: 14).

The folk-memory of an actual flood may have contributed something to the story, but there is no geological evidence of a flood of such magnitude as that described in Genesis, in which 'every living thing that existed on earth, man and beast, reptile and bird . . . were all wiped out over the whole earth, and only Noah and his company in the ark survived' (Gen. 7: 23). Archaeologists have found 'clean water-laid clay' (C. L. Woolley) at various depths in several areas in the Tigris–Euphrates valley (map **4**), and this may be evidence of considerable local flooding having taken place at a number of different times. In the diagram (**18**) the shaded layers represent strata which may be flood deposits. Deposit A found at Erech by J. Jordan in 1929 is 1·5 metres (about 4 ft 11 in.) thick; deposit B found at Ur by C. L. Woolley in 1929 is from 3·7 to 2·7 metres (about 12 ft to 8 ft 9 in.) thick; deposit C found at Kish by S. Langdon in 1930 is 0·5 metre (about 1 ft 8 in.) thick, and has three thinner deposits below it; deposit D found at Nineveh by R. C. Thompson and M. E. L. Mallowan in 1932 is 1·8 metres (about 6 ft) thick; and deposit E found at Shuruppak by E. Schmidt in 1931 is 0·6 metre (about 2 ft) thick. The photograph (**19**) shows part of the deposit at Ur, and the locations of the places where deposits have been found are indicated on the map (**4**).

Tower of Babel

Early man's questioning about the languages spoken in different localities (p. 25) is answered in Genesis by the story of the tower of Babel. It tells of a plan to build 'a city and a tower with its top in the heavens', and how God punished this arrogance by scattering the builders 'all over the face of the earth' so that 'they left off building the city'. The unfinished city was given the name Babel (N.E.B. footnote: '*That is* Babylon') 'because the LORD there made a babble of the language of all the world' (Gen. 11: 1–9). Many artists have been attracted by this subject, Peter Breughel the Elder (1520–69) among them (**20**). This picture in the Vienna Museum shows the building operations in full swing.

20 *The Tower of Babel, Peter Breughel, Vienna Museum*

Towers surmounted by temples have been excavated at several places, particularly in Mesopotamia (map **4**). They are called ziggurats, and they probably represent man's attempt to establish contact between earth and heaven. The ziggurat at Ur will be described later (pp. 31f.). The magnificent ziggurat that once stood in the city of Babylon (map **4**) may have given the original writer the idea for his story of the tower of Babel. One of the wonders of the ancient world, it is described in cuneiform (that is, wedge-shaped writing; for example, **13**) on a clay tablet now in the Louvre, Paris. According to this account, the tower had seven storeys, a base about 90 metres (295 feet) square, and a total height of about 90 metres. It was still standing in Nebuchadnezzar's day, for one of his inscriptions records his repair of it. This model of the ziggurat at Babylon (**21**) is in the Oriental Institute of the University of Chicago.

21 *Model of the ziggurat at Babylon*

2.   PATRIARCHAL PERIOD

Abraham

According to Gen. 11: 28, 31 Abraham may have been born at 'Ur of the Chaldees', but in the Greek version of the Old Testament, the Septuagint (pp. 144f.), those verses speak only of 'the land of the Chaldees' and do not mention Ur specifically. There is also some uncertainty about the location of Ur, and many sites have been suggested. Excavation seems to support the view, however, that the ruins which now stand about 16 kilometres (10 miles) west of the present course of the Euphrates (the river has changed its course from time to time) are the remains of the city of Ur named in Genesis (map **4**). This aerial view of Ur (**22**) shows the extent of the city and the orderly arrangement of its streets. The

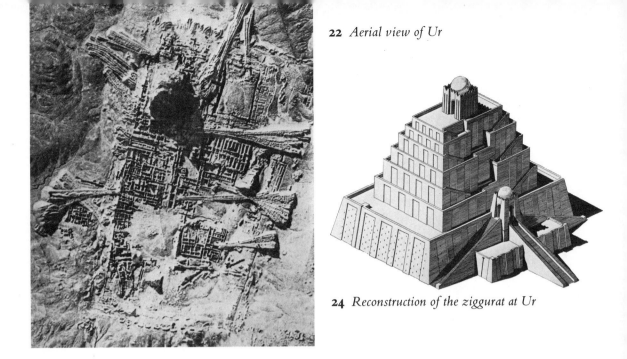

22 *Aerial view of Ur*

24 *Reconstruction of the ziggurat at Ur*

site is dominated by an artificial mound made of solid brickwork, seen in dark shadow in the middle of the photograph. A nearer view (**23**) shows this to be the remains of a ziggurat with three stairways each of one hundred steps by which the temple at its summit was approached. The god worshipped at Ur was Nanna, the moon god. The ziggurat was thoroughly excavated by C. L. Woolley during his exploration of Ur between 1922 and 1934. The fan-shaped banks are dumps of excavated earth brought by light railway from the ruins. Woolley's suggested restoration of the ziggurat (**24**) shows something of the impressive splendour it must have had in its heyday.

23 *The ziggurat at Ur*

The bricks on the outside surface of the ziggurat are glazed and coloured; those inside are unglazed. The structure had fallen into ruins by the sixth century B.C., and it was splendidly restored by Nabonidus, king of Babylon from 555 to 539 B.C. He buried inscribed cylinders of baked clay in the corners of the restored mound, on which were described the rebuilding of the ziggurat and on which the city is identified. C. L. Woolley's excavation of Ur unearthed many remarkable and beautiful objects, several of which are to be seen in the Babylonian Room of the British Museum and some of which are illustrated elsewhere in this book (**10, 132**).

25 *Abraham, Donatello, Campanile del Duomo, Florence*

This statue (**25**) by Donatello (1383–1466) shows a most impressive portrait of Abraham. He is being 'put . . . to the test' by God, and he has already 'built an altar and arranged the wood', and taken the knife to kill Isaac, his son. He is perhaps looking toward the 'ram caught by its horns in a thicket', which in the story he 'offered . . . as a sacrifice instead of his son' (Gen. 22: 1–14). The statue is in the Campanile del Duomo, Florence.

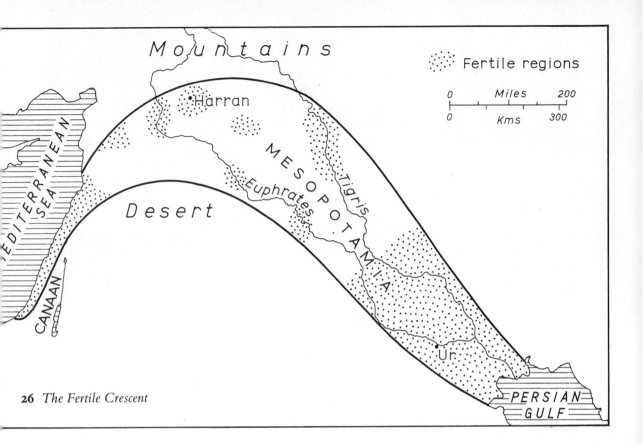

26 *The Fertile Crescent*

The Fertile Crescent

This map (**26**) shows the region with which the patriarchs are associated in the Bible. It includes the Tigris–Euphrates valley and the coastal strip of Canaan, which together form a nearly semi-circular belt of mainly fertile land known today as the Fertile Crescent. To north and south of it the countryside is barren and unsuitable for human habitation. Mesopotamia (meaning literally 'between the rivers') was one of the cradles of civilization, and it was here, according to the biblical account, that Abraham lived before his migration to Canaan. He and his family 'set out from Ur of the Chaldees' and 'when they reached Harran, they settled there' (Gen. 11: 30f.).

Mari

In 1933 a headless statue was dug up during quarrying operations at a place now identified as the royal city of Mari (map **4**). This discovery was considered to be an important one and it brought André Parrot and his team of French archaeologists to the site, and excavation began in the same year. The work went on until the outbreak of World War II in 1939, and it was resumed in 1951 and continued until 1956. It was richly rewarded. Parrot unearthed a ziggurat, several important

27 *Aerial view of Mari*

temples, and an enormous royal palace. This aerial photograph (**27**) gives some idea of the great size of the palace. It had about 300 rooms, some of them decorated with fine wall paintings and many of them containing superb examples of Mesopotamian art. The palace kitchen was so well preserved when Parrot discovered it that he says 'it could have been put into use at once'. Above and to the left of the palace in this aerial view are to be seen the excavated temple of Ishtar and its surrounding buildings. Lengths of light railway track can be distinguished. The railway was used to remove the soil dug out during the excavations, and the fan-shaped embankments at the ends of the tracks are dumps of this soil.

The most significant find from our point of view was the palace library of about 20,000 cuneiform clay tablets written in the eighteenth century B.C. They include business contracts, lists of people and materials, accounts, and public and private correspondence; but it is the descriptions they give of customs in northern Mesopotamia that are important, because they throw so much light on the period to which the patriarchs are probably to be ascribed. Similar tablets of about the same period found at Nuzi (map **4**) add greatly to our knowledge of these customs. The tablets found at Mari and at Nuzi describe incidents that are strikingly similar to some in the Bible that we might otherwise find difficult to understand. Three examples from the stories of the patriarchs may be quoted. (i) Because Sarai was not able at that time to have children, she gave 'an Egyptian slave-girl whose name was Hagar . . . to her husband Abram as a wife' (Gen. 16: 1–3). (ii) The birthright was the treasured possession of the eldest son in a family, yet Esau 'swore an oath and sold his birthright to Jacob' for a bowl of lentil broth (Gen. 25: 33). (iii) Rachel, Laban's daughter, 'stole her father's household gods', but 'Jacob did not know that Rachel had stolen the gods'. He said to

Laban 'Whoever is found in possession of your gods shall die for it' (Gen. 31: 19–35). In the light of the discoveries at Mari and Nuzi these incidents are seen to reflect practices and ideas that were common in northern Mesopotamia during the patriarchal period.

Hammurabi's code

During excavations carried out in 1901–2 at Susa (map **4**), 'the capital city' of king Ahasuerus 'who ruled from India to Ethiopia' (Esther 1: 1f.), Jacques de Morgan, a French archaeologist, found three broken parts of a stele (that is, an inscribed pillar). When the pieces were fitted together by expert craftsmen (a joint can be seen in the photograph) there appeared an impressive black stone monument 2·25 metres (about 7 feet) high (**28**). It is covered with cuneiform writing, except for the upper section which depicts a king standing before an enthroned god who is offering a sceptre and a ring to the king as the signs of his royal authority. Scholars think that the god is Shamash, the sun god (**175**), and that the king is Hammurabi, ruler of Babylon from 1728 to 1686 B.C. The cuneiform writing is a list of laws drawn up by Hammurabi; originally 280 of them, but some of them appear to have been deliberately erased.

Hammurabi probably had this pillar erected in the temple of Marduk in his capital city of Babylon, but it was removed several centuries later as a trophy of

28 *Hammurabi's code*

war at the time of Babylon's decline in power. It is now one of the most treasured possessions in the Louvre, Paris.

At least five other ancient lists of laws written on clay tablets have been discovered since the finding of Hammurabi's code, all of them, like Hammurabi's, earlier than the laws in the Old Testament. Hammurabi's laws have particularly close connections with the laws in Exod. 21–3, often called the 'Book of the Covenant'. There are interesting similarities in all the lists, and the dependence of later lists on earlier ones must be assumed. There are also differences. For example, the Israelite code states the law of retaliation thus: 'Wherever hurt is done, you shall give life for life, eye for eye, tooth for tooth, hand for hand, foot for foot, burn for burn, bruise for bruise, wound for wound' (Exod. 21:23–5). Hammurabi's law of retaliation is almost identical with this, but the other early codes differ from it. They impose fines or require compensation for bodily injuries.

29 *Jacob's Dream, A. Straehuber*

Jacob

In this engraving (**29**) by A. Straehuber (1814–83) Jacob has taken a large stone and 'made it a pillow for his head' and has fallen asleep. In his dream he sees 'a ladder, which rested on the ground with its top reaching to heaven', shown here as a stairway with 'angels of God . . . going up and down upon it'. The figure of God floats above the angels, although in the biblical account of the incident 'the LORD was standing beside' Jacob (Gen. 28:10–17).

The river Jabbok (map **1**), a tributary of the Jordan, flows in a meandering course from the mountains of Gilead in the east (**30**), joining the Jordan about 37 kilometres (23 miles) north of the Dead Sea. In Old Testament times it served as a

30 *River Jabbok*

convenient frontier between the Amorite kingdom of Sihon and the territory of the Ammonites in the period before the settlement of the Israelites in Canaan; and between the half tribe of Manasseh and the tribe of Gad after the settlement. It was when Jacob was crossing 'the ford of Jabbok' that 'a man wrestled with him there till daybreak', and Jacob's name was changed to Israel (Gen. 32:22–32). His descendants thereafter were called 'Israelites' or 'the children of Israel', until the exile. After the exile they were called, as they are today, 'Jews' because of their link with Judah (the Hebrew words for 'Jew' and 'Judah' are very nearly the same).

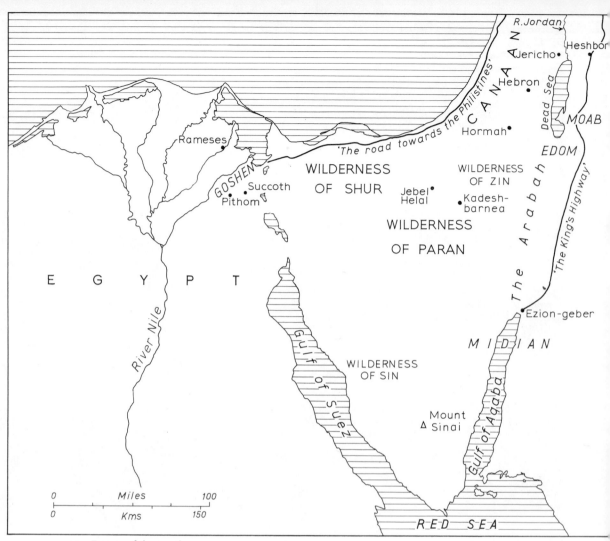

31 *Route of the exodus*

3. THE EXODUS (map **31**)

The route taken by the Israelites, probably in the thirteenth century B.C., on their journey from Egypt to Canaan cannot be shown with certainty on a map. Place names occur in plenty in the biblical accounts of the exodus, but the locations of many of them are not known. The journey began 'in the land of Goshen, where the Israelites lived' (Exod. 9: 26), and where 'they were made to work in gangs with officers set over them, to break their spirit with heavy labour' building 'Pharaoh's store-cities, Pithom and Rameses' (Exod. 1: 11).

The shortest way from Goshen to Canaan is along the caravan and military road that skirts the coast, known when the book of Exodus was written (p. 137) as 'the road towards the Philistines' (Exod. 13: 17). This important road certainly existed in the thirteenth century B.C., but that could not then have been its name, for the Philistines did not settle in these parts until nearly a century later. This coast road was strongly guarded by Egyptian frontier posts, which made it an impossible escape route for the Israelites. None of these outposts can now be identified with certainty, but they are named on a bas-relief at Karnak (map **3**). Prevented from travelling by this route, the Israelites may have gone along the narrow sandy causeway in the sea to the north of the Egyptian mainland (map **31**). It seems more probable, however, that they went 'by stages as the LORD told them' (Exod. 17: 1) in a south-easterly direction, perhaps from Rameses to Succoth, then skirting the wilderness of Sin to arrive eventually at Mount Sinai in the south of the Sinai peninsula.

This part of the journey, by whatever route, included a miraculous sea crossing and the drowning of the pursuing Egyptian army (p. 48). The sea is named in an ancient poem, which says that 'the chariots of Pharaoh and his army', with 'the flower of his officers' were 'engulfed in the Red Sea' (Exod. 15: 4). It is not necessary, however, to believe that the references to 'the Red Sea' in the accounts of the exodus are to the Red Sea shown on a modern map (map **3**). As suggested in footnote (*b*) to Exod. 10: 19 in the New English Bible, the Hebrew words mean 'Sea of Reeds', and a narrow extension of one of the marshy lakes north of the Gulf of Suez (now part of the Suez Canal) may have been the place of crossing.

From Sinai 'the Israelites moved by stages' until they reached 'the wilderness of Paran' (Num. 10: 12), encamping at several places on the way. Ezion-geber is named as one of their stopping places (Num. 33: 35). Eventually, 'the whole community of Israel reached the wilderness of Zin and stayed some time at Kadesh' (Num. 20: 1). This place is sometimes (e.g. Num. 32: 8) called Kadesh-barnea to distinguish it from other places called Kadesh. Moses sent spies from Kadesh 'to explore the land of Canaan' (Num. 13: 17). They penetrated as far as Hebron and brought back a favourable account of the land, together with a warning about the difficulty of capturing it. 'It is flowing with milk and honey', they said, 'but its inhabitants are sturdy, and the cities are very strongly fortified' (Num. 13: 27f.).

'From Kadesh Moses sent envoys to the king of Edom' (Num. 20: 14) seeking permission for the Israelites to pass through his territory, promising that they would 'keep to the king's highway' (Num. 20: 17). The king's highway was an ancient road running from Ezion-geber on the Gulf of Aqaba in the south to Damascus in the north (map **31**), passing through the hill-country to the east of the Jordan Valley. It was a busy caravan route used for the export of precious perfumes from Arabia. A railway follows roughly the same route today. Permission to use this road was refused, so 'Israel went a different way to avoid a conflict' (Num. 20: 21). A rebellious few tried to enter Canaan in spite of the Edomite refusal of permission, going 'recklessly on their way towards the heights of the hill-country' (Num: 14: 44), but this foolhardy venture was repelled at a decisive battle at Hormah.

The next stage of the journey took the Israelites 'round the flank of Edom' (Num. 21: 4) to encamp 'in the wilderness on the eastern frontier of Moab' (Num. 21: 11). Again they sought permission, this time from king Sihon, to use the king's highway, and again it was refused, but the Israelites successfully attacked the people of Sihon's territory and 'occupied their land from the Arnon to the Jabbok' (map 1), settling in 'Heshbon and all its dependent villages' (Num. 21: 24f.). Heshbon (map 31) was Sihon's capital city. The Israelites now pushed north, encountering and defeating the army of Og, the gigantic king of Bashan (map 1) whose 'sarcophagus of basalt was nearly fourteen feet long and six feet wide' (Deut. 3: 11), capturing sixty 'fortified cities with high walls, gates, and bars' and 'a great many open settlements' (Deut. 3: 5).

Israel now encamped on the east side of Jordan opposite Jericho, and by crossing the river at a time when the flow of the stream was held back they invaded Canaan, thus reaching the end of their long journey from Egypt to the promised land.

There are many uncertain features about the route described above. For example, did the Israelites travel from Ezion-geber along the Arabah, the dry valley which extends southward beyond the Jordan Valley, or by a route east of the king's highway? Did they go to Sinai by way of the wilderness of Sin, or did they go eastward from Succoth to Kadesh-barnea by way of the wilderness of Shur, Mount Sinai in that case being identified with Jebel Helal (map 31), a mountain about 35 kilometres (22 miles) west of Kadesh-barnea?

The details of the exodus journey are complex, and the descriptions of it in Exodus, Numbers, and Deuteronomy are not always consistent. The danger of over-simplification is always present in any attempt to reconstruct the route, but in any case the geographical features of the exodus are of little consequence in comparison with its religious significance.

Thutmose III

Thutmose III was the Egyptian Pharaoh from about 1482 to 1450 B.C., probably when the Israelites were slaves in Egypt. An inscription in the temple of Amon at Karnak (map 3) gives some indication of his might (32). He is represented as holding a batch of prisoners by the hair and about to smite them. (His right arm is missing, but the attitude of smiting is a conventional one, well known from many other inscriptions in which the right arm is shown.) The prisoners are

32 *Thutmose III inscription at Karnak*

kneeling, holding up their hands and pleading for mercy. To the right a goddess leads by a rope a group of conquered chieftains, and below the figure of Thutmose there are three more rows of captives. In the upper right-hand corner there is a damaged representation of the god Amon.

Each human figure in the groups of captives probably represents a city or an area conquered by Thutmose. The localities are named in hieroglyphics within the ring-shapes which hide the legs of the figures. A similar feature is found on the base of the statue of Rameses II at Luxor (**35**). These symbols represent in a graphic form the enormous political and military power of the Pharaohs in the centuries immediately before the exodus.

Tell el-Amarna Letters
Amenhotep IV became Pharaoh of Egypt in about 1380 B.C. He was a young man full of reforming zeal, but the time and energy he expended in reforming

Egyptian religion resulted in the serious neglect of his political duties. His enemies took advantage of the situation and much of the empire was eventually lost. Amenhotep dismissed a host of Egyptian gods and goddesses and instituted the worship of one god, Aten, in honour of whom he changed his own name to Akhen-aten. He also moved his capital from Thebes to Amarna about 420 kilometres (261 miles) lower down the Nile (map 3), where he established his palace and a temple to Aten. The mound now covering the ancient ruins of this place is called Tell el-Amarna.

In 1887 a peasant woman digging at Tell el-Amarna accidentally unearthed a large collection of clay tablets covered with cuneiform writing, which she sold to a neighbour for a very small sum. They turned out to be extremely valuable and 82 of them eventually found their way to the British Museum, and others went to museums in Berlin and Cairo. They are letters written in the fourteenth century B.C. between kings of small city states in several parts of western Asia and the Pharaohs of Egypt, Akhen-aten and his father. They tell us a great deal about the state of affairs just before the exodus. Evidently the political and military situation was out of control, Egyptian power was rapidly waning, and bands of outlaws called Habiru were overrunning the land. The Tell el-Amarna letters call upon Egypt for help to repel the Habiru; help which by this time she was probably incapable of giving.

The letter illustrated here (33) is one of nine sent from Gezer (map 1), and one of the three sent by Yapahi, a king of Gezer, asking for Egyptian assistance at a time when the city was being attacked.

33 *A letter from Tell el-Amarna*

34 *Inscriptions at Karnak*

Rameses II

The date of the exodus from Egypt is not known with certainty, but it was probably in the thirteenth century B.C., a period about which the monuments left behind by the Pharaohs tell us a great deal. At both Luxor and Karnak, which now occupy roughly the site of Thebes (map **3**), the ancient capital of Egypt, there are magnificent remains of royal temples and palaces. Inscriptions on the walls (**34**) are contemporary records of events in the history of Egypt.

Rameses II was Pharaoh of Egypt from about 1290 to 1224 B.C., and there is an enormous statue of him in the temple at Luxor (**35**). On the base of this statue there is a list of the places conquered by Rameses, and a row of prisoners tied together by ropes round their necks.

35 *Statue of Rameses II at Luxor*

36 *Statue of Rameses II probably from Karnak*

A granite statue of Rameses II (**36**) which probably once stood in the temple at Karnak is now in the museum at Turin. It shows him seated, a symbolic serpent on the front of his helmet and a sceptre in his hand, signs of his royal authority.

The processional avenue near the temple at Karnak (**37**) was constructed by Rameses II. It is flanked on either side by rows of ram-headed sphinxes, each of their heads supported by small figures of the Pharaoh.

37 *Processional avenue at Karnak*

38 *Inscriptions near the Dog River*

Dog River inscription

The right-hand side inscription of the two shown here (**38**) was erected by Rameses II to commemorate his campaigns against the Hittites, who were gradually encroaching on the Egyptian empire. The left-hand side inscription is much later, and it depicts an unknown king, probably engaged in worship. The inscriptions are cut in the solid rock near Dog River north of Beirut (map **3**). The mountains come down to the sea and the river cuts through the rock to empty into the Mediterranean Sea. The Dog River formed the northern boundary of the Egyptian empire, and in his campaign against the Hittites Rameses II crossed it without difficulty. He was the first of many conquerors to commemorate his victory by erecting an inscription here.

Moses

This gigantic figure of Moses (**39**) is perhaps the most famous of all Michelangelo's sculptures. Under his right arm Moses holds 'the two tablets of the Tokens, tablets of stone written with the finger of God' (Exod. 31: 18). From the curly hair on Moses' head are projecting the two horns which tradition ascribes to him. The Hebrew words for 'shine' and 'horn' are nearly alike (*qaran* and *qeren*). Most translators have assumed that *qaran* was the word in the original and have said that Moses 'did not know that the skin of his face shone' when he came down from Mount Sinai (Exod. 34: 29). Jerome, however, assumed that *qeren* was the word in the original, and in the Vulgate (p. 145) he says that Moses 'knew not that his face was horned'. That is why some artists familiar only with the Vulgate have represented Moses with horns. The original of this statue is in the church of San Pietro in Vincolo, Rome, but a cast of it may be seen in the South Kensington Museum, London.

This fresco (**40**) by Botticelli (1445–1510) in the Sistine Chapel of the Vatican, Rome, is a composite picture illustrating incidents in the life of Moses. The following are seen in the various sections of the picture: an Egyptian striking an Israelite, and Moses revenging this attack on one of his kinsmen (Exod. 2: 11–15); Moses tending the flock of his father-in-law, Jethro, priest of Midian (Exod. 3: 1); Moses taking off his sandals because he recognized that he was on holy ground, and then kneeling before the bush that was on fire but was not burnt up (Exod. 3: 1–5); Moses carrying his staff, leading the Israelites through the wilderness, with manna (pp. 51f.), the 'bread' that was their food when they were on the march, on the ground (Exod. 15: 22 – 16: 19).

40 *Scenes in the Life of Moses, Botticelli, Sistine Chapel*

Crossing the Red Sea

This fresco (**41**) is the work of Piero di Cosimo (1462–1521), a pupil of Cosimo Rosselli (1439–1507) after whom he is named. Both master and pupil worked under Botticelli on the decoration of the Sistine Chapel in the Vatican, Rome. The work was completed in 1474, and this painting occupies one panel of it. The subject is the crossing of the Red Sea. The Israelites on the left of the picture are on dry land. Moses, their leader, holds the staff he was told to stretch over the sea to 'cleave it in two' (Exod. 14: 16). On the right 'all Pharaoh's army, the chariots and the cavalry' are floundering in the sea that has been made to 'flow back over the Egyptians' (Exod. 14: 26, 28).

41 *Crossing the Red Sea, Piero di Cosimo, Sistine Chapel*

42 *Jebel Musa*

Mount Sinai

The location of Mount Sinai (so called in J and P, but called Horeb in E and D: see pp. 137f.) is uncertain, but this drawing (**42**) is of the mountain traditionally associated with the exodus story. It is the highest peak (modern name, Jebel Musa) in a range of hills in the south of the Sinai peninsula (map **31**). This mountain is not volcanic, and because some readers of the Bible detect the suggestion that Sinai was an active volcano they place it elsewhere. In favour of their opinion they quote Exod. 19: 18; 'Mount Sinai was all smoking . . . the smoke went up like the smoke of a kiln', and Exod. 13: 21, which mentions 'a pillar of cloud' and 'a pillar of fire', though in the latter case the phenomena are not specifically associated with the mountain. Jebel Helal near Kadesh (map **31**; see also p. 40) is sometimes suggested. It is not difficult to imagine the events described in Exodus 19 taking place at the foot of the awe-inspiring 'mount of God' (1 Kings 19: 8) seen in this picture.

The Wilderness

The Israelites travelled through 'difficult country' (Exod. 14: 3) on their way to the promised land, crossing vast areas where the scenery is monotonous and where travel is hazardous. In springtime there may be a sparse covering of grass, just sufficient to support a few sheep; but for most of the year the streams are dried up, rainfall is negligible in quantity, and vegetation is burnt up by the scorching sun. Conditions vary considerably from year to year, but droughts of great severity are not uncommon.

43 *Aerial view of the Jordan Valley*

This aerial view of the Jordan Valley looking north (**43**), and the closer view of part of the same area east of Jordan near the Dead Sea (**44**), show these features clearly. Deep ravines run into the Jordan Valley from the east, and one of these, the Jabbok Valley (**30**), appears near the bottom of the picture. Scanty vegetation

44 *The wilderness near the Dead Sea*

can be seen on the picture giving the closer view (**44**). It is not surprising that, living in this environment, 'the people complained to Moses' about the shortage of drinking water (Exod. 15: 24), and the lack of food that might make the 'whole assembly starve to death' (Exod. 16: 2f.), or that 'the whole Israelite community cried out in dismay; all night long they wept' because of the severity of the conditions (Num. 14: 1).

Mount Nebo (map **1**) is beyond the hills in the distance (**44**). It was from the summit of this mountain, 'the top of Pisgah' (Pisgah is the highest peak in the Nebo range of mountains), that Moses was allowed to see 'the whole land' that had been promised to the Israelites; and it was in this area, 'in the land of Moab', that 'Moses the servant of the LORD died', and where 'he was buried in a valley', although 'to this day no one knows his burial-place' (Deut. 34: 1–6).

Manna

When the Israelites travelling from Egypt to Canaan reached the wilderness of Sin (map **31**) they were short of food. They complained bitterly to Moses, fearing they might 'starve to death', and in answer to their complaint 'bread from heaven' was given to them. Next morning, 'when the dew was gone', there appeared 'fine flakes, . . . fine as hoar-frost on the ground'. They gathered it, each of them 'just as much as he could eat'. It was 'white, like coriander seed, and it tasted like a wafer made with honey'. 'Israel called the food manna' (Exod. 16: 2–31).

If a natural explanation of this episode is required, there are several suggestions available. Various insects suck the sap of certain plants that grow in desert regions, and then exude a sweet-tasting substance which bears some resemblance to the substance described above. This rare photograph (**45**) was taken by F. S. Boden-heimer, a botanist of the Hebrew University, Jerusalem, during an expedition in the region of Mount Sinai in 1927. It shows twigs of a tamarisk bush on which najacocci (plant-lice) have deposited globules of a glassy substance which is collected and eaten by the Bedouin of the Sinai Peninsula. It is said that in a good

45 *Exudation from najacocci on a tamarisk bush*

season a man can easily gather a kilogram (about 2·2 pounds) of this exudation in a day. It may be the substance the Israelites gathered and ate, calling it manna (Hebrew: *man-hu*, which means, 'What is that?'. See the footnote to Exod. 16: 15 in the New English Bible).

4. CONQUEST AND SETTLEMENT

Conquest

According to one account, that in the book of Joshua, the conquest of Canaan by the Israelites was speedy, ferocious, and complete. According to another account, that in the book of Judges, it was long drawn out, and only partially successful. It was evidently a complex operation, consisting partly of guerilla warfare, partly of well-planned campaigns, and perhaps partly also of peaceful infiltration.

Moses commanded the Israelites to go to Gilgal (map **1**) when they had crossed the Jordan and entered Canaan, and on Mount Gerizim to 'pronounce the blessing and on Mount Ebal the curse' (Deut. 11: 29), 'the whole of the blessing and the cursing word by word, as they are written in the book of the law' (Josh. 8: 34). In this picture (**46**) the two mountains are seen. Gerizim on the left and Ebal on the right. Nablus, which has replaced the ancient city of Shechem (map **1**) but not on exactly the same site, lies between them in the plain. After the fall of the northern kingdom of Israel (p. 73), Shechem became the chief city of the Samaritans, 'the senseless folk that live at Sechem' (Ecclus. 50: 26), and there is still a small community of Samaritans at Nablus today. The houses on the extreme left of the picture are modern.

46 *Mount Gerizim and Mount Ebal*

Philistines

At about the same time as the Israelites entered Canaan by crossing the Jordan from the east (p. 40), the Philistines invaded the country from the south and settled on the coastal plain in an area later known as Philistia (map **3**). Although they were not Semites (p. 122) and were despised by the Hebrews as 'the uncircumcised Philistines' (Judg. 14: 3), they eventually gave their name in a modified form (Palestine) to the whole country.

Clashes between the Israelites and the Philistines were inevitable, and in the period of the early monarchy the Philistines were victorious, perhaps because they had a monopoly in iron weapons and chariots, whereas 'no blacksmith was to be found in the whole of Israel' (1 Sam. 13: 19). David finally defeated the Philistines, but they continued to be a thorn in the side of Israel during the period of the divided monarchy. Even in the time of Isaiah the 'Philistines from the west' are said to have 'swallowed Israel in one mouthful' (Isa. 9: 12).

The illustration (**47**) shows some of the captives taken by Rameses III. The second prisoner from the right is a Philistine. He wears the characteristic dress of a warrior: a kilt with tassels, and a curious head-dress with a chin-strap and a crown of plumes probably made of horsehair. The captives from left to right are Libyan, Semite, Hittite, Philistine, and another Semite. They are strung together by the neck. This bas-relief is on a wall of the mortuary temple built by Rameses III at Medinet Habu on the outskirts of Thebes (map **3**).

47 *Philistine warrior*

48 *Samson and the Lion, Albrecht Dürer*

The judges

The judges were local hero–leaders who sprang into prominence in this period because of their military skill and their ability to rally the Israelite forces when a crisis arose. The exploits of thirteen of them are described in the book of Judges, but it is Samson who is the most popular as a subject for pictorial representation. He is reputed to have been supernaturally strong, and in this woodcut (**48**) by Albrecht Dürer (1471–1528) he is shown in the act of killing a lion with his hands. It was at Timnath that 'a young lion came at him growling' and that 'having no weapon in his hand, he tore the lion in pieces as if it were a kid' (Judg. 14: 5f.).

In this picture (**49**) by Rubens (1577–1640) in the Alte Pinakothek, Munich, Samson is breaking loose from the Philistines who are trying to secure him. Delilah, with whom Samson is in love, has taken 'the seven loose locks' of

49 *Samson Taken Prisoner, Rubens, Alte Pinakothek, Munich*

Samson's hair and woven them on a loom to make a strong rope with which she has bound him. Such is his strength, however, that when the Philistines come to take him he pulls off the rope 'and the loom with it' and so escapes (Judg. 16: 13–16). In the picture Delilah still has the shears in her hand, and Samson's hair is shown cut short.

The capture of Jericho

Jericho stands in a key position, defending the Jordan Valley and the important passes leading to the west and to the coast (map **1**). Its capture was therefore essential to Joshua if his army was to penetrate further into Canaan. 'Jericho was bolted and barred' against attack, however, and its conquest presented very great difficulty to the unarmed Israelites. The Bible describes the strategy by which the city was captured (Josh. 6: 1–21).

This modern drawing (**50**) by Carel Weight (born 1908) gives the artist's impression of the attack on the city. 'Seven priests . . . carrying seven trumpets made from rams' horns' were told to march round the city, 'making the circuit of it once, for six days running', but 'on the seventh day' they were to march 'seven times round the city in the same way'. On the seventh circuit 'the priests blew the trumpets . . . the army . . . raised a great shout, and down fell the walls'. Following Joshua's orders, 'they then set fire to the city and everything in it' and 'put everyone to the sword, men and women, young and old' (Josh. 6: 1–26). The drawing shows the priests blowing their trumpets with considerable enthusiasm (one of them, in the bottom left-hand corner of the picture, has given up, unable to stand the din), and the walls tottering.

50 *The Capture of Jericho, Carel Weight*

In 1930, J. Garstang claimed to have unearthed the walls of Jericho destroyed by Joshua's army, together with evidence of the burning of the city: the effect of fire on the walls, and charred remains of dates, barley, olives, bread, and unbaked dough. More recent investigation and further excavation carried out between 1952 and 1958 by Miss Kathleen Kenyon have shown Garstang to be mistaken. The walls he found are something like 1,000 years earlier than the period of the conquest of Canaan, and no trace of the walls destroyed by Joshua has been discovered. Ancient Jericho was probably quite small and the remains of it may have been washed away by erosion and the stone taken away and used for building purposes elsewhere.

Neither Joshua nor the judges succeeded in capturing the whole of Canaan. The Israelites were generally successful in the hill-country (although Jerusalem was not captured), but some of the plain-dwellers had 'chariots of iron' (Judg. 1: 19) and were more than a match for the Israelites. Among these plain-dwellers were 'those in the Vale of Jezreel' (Josh. 17: 16). This great plain (map **1**), also called the Plain of Esdraelon ('Esdraelon' is a Greek modification of 'Jezreel'), is the only break of any size in the range of hills running the length of Palestine to the west of the Jordan Valley (map **1**, diagram **2**). In this photograph (**51**) it is shown as it appears when looking from west to east. Mount Tabor is in the distance, and there is a plantation of young trees in the foreground.

51 *The Vale of Jezreel from the west*

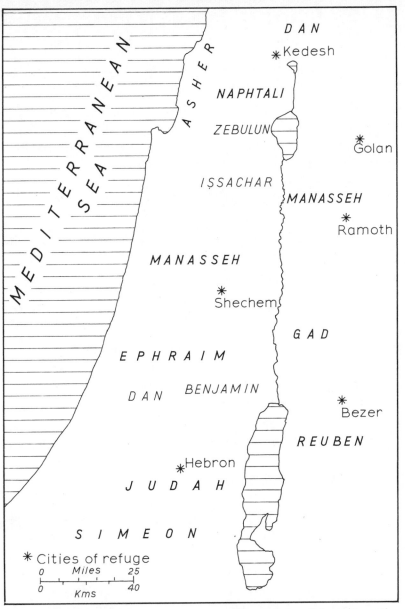

52 *The territory of the twelve tribes*

The twelve tribes

Jacob had twelve sons, and it was these sons and their households who went to Egypt and settled in Goshen. By the end of the period of slavery in Egypt these twelve households had become twelve tribes, and when they returned to Canaan they occupied separate territory (map **52**). Of the twelve original tribes, Joseph was subdivided to form the tribes of Manasseh and Ephraim, probably because Levi was the ancestor of a priestly class rather than of a tribe, and it was important to keep the number of tribes at twelve. At some stage Simeon was merged with

Judah, for we hear nothing of the tribe of Simeon when Rehoboam is named as king of the southern kingdom formed by the union of the tribes of Judah and Benjamin. Nevertheless, the two merged tribes continued to be counted separately so as to maintain the number twelve. Half the tribe of Manasseh were given permission to share with Gad and Reuben the rich land to the east of Jordan, and the other half of the tribe eventually settled in central Canaan to the west of the Jordan. Even after its division, Manasseh counted as one tribe. Dan originally occupied territory in the south, but they were harassed by the Amorites and forced into the hills. Spies sent to explore the extreme north reported favourably and the tribe of Dan 'marched against Leshem, attacked it and captured it'. They 'renamed the place Dan' (map **1**) and settled there (Josh. 19: 47).

Cities of refuge

Before they crossed the Jordan into Canaan, Moses instructed the Israelites to 'designate certain cities to be places of refuge, in which the homicide who has killed a man by accident may take sanctuary'. They were to be 'six in number, three east of the Jordan and three in Canaan' (Num. 35: 11–15); that is, they were to be so distributed in the land that no place in it was far from one of them (map **52**). An example is given of 'the kind of homicide who may take sanctuary': 'the man who goes into a wood with his mate to fell trees, and, when cutting a tree, he relaxes his grip on the axe, the head glances off the tree, hits the other man and kills him' (Deut. 19: 4f.).

A murderer could be attacked and killed on his way to a city of refuge, but once he had reached the city he had to be given a fair trial, and only if he were proved guilty of wilful murder could he be put to death by 'the dead man's next-of-kin' (Num. 35: 19). If the attacker killed a man 'on the spur of the moment . . . not of set purpose' he must stay in the city of refuge 'till the death of the duly anointed high priest' and be protected 'from the vengeance of the kinsman'. After that he is free to 'go back to his property' (Num. 35: 16–29).

5.   THE UNITED MONARCHY

Saul

The exact boundaries of Saul's kingdom are not known with certainty, but the shaded areas on this map (**53**) suggest the approximate extent of the kingdom at the end of his reign.

Saul, 'a young man in his prime . . . a head taller than any of his fellows' (1 Sam. 9: 2), was anointed by Samuel to 'rule the people of the LORD and deliver them from the enemies round about them' (1 Sam. 10: 1). His royal authority was recognized at Mizpah where the crowd 'all acclaimed him, shouting, "Long live the king!"' (1 Sam. 10: 24). Saul's court was established at Gibeah.

Saul's victory over the Ammonites at Jabesh-gilead secured for him an area of land east of the Jordan, and his victory over the Philistines in the early years of his reign gave him land to the west of the river. He never succeeded in capturing Jerusalem, but he gained pockets of territory in the south, where he 'cut the Amalekites to pieces' and 'destroyed all the people, putting them to the sword' (1 Sam. 15: 7f.). Saul died in battle against the Philistines on Mount Gilboa.

David

David was first made ruler of his own tribe, Judah, and he and his followers 'settled in the city of Hebron' (2 Sam. 2: 3f.). Later he became king of all Israel, captured Jerusalem (p. 62), and 'took up his residence in the stronghold and called it the City of David' (2 Sam. 5: 9). David conducted successful campaigns against the Philistines, the Moabites, the Aramaeans of Damascus, the Ammonites, the Edomites and the Amalekites. He made a treaty with Hiram, king of Tyre, and thus gained a measure of control over Phoenicia. The shaded areas on the map (**54**) show the approximate extent of David's kingdom at its greatest. It reached the

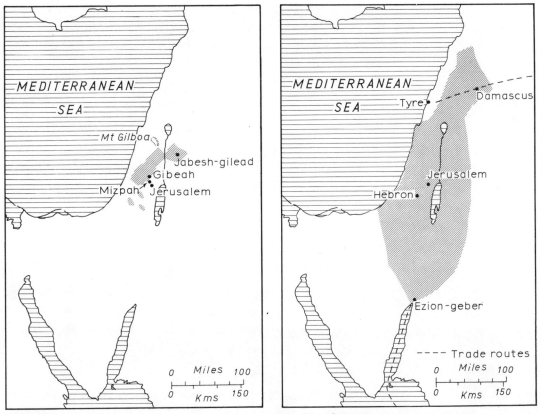

53 *Saul's territory*   **54** *David's territory*

limits promised to the descendants of Abraham; 'from the River of Egypt to the Great River, the river Euphrates' (Gen. 15:18). The 'River of Egypt' was a stream on the eastern border of Egypt.

The capture of Edom gave David possession of Ezion-geber and control of the Red Sea route to the south. His conquest of Syria gave him control of an important overland trade route from the Mediterranean coast to Damascus and the Middle East. David thus had splendid opportunities to develop profitable commercial activities, but it was not until the reign of Solomon that these were fully exploited.

David and Goliath

In one of the best known of David's youthful deeds of bravery, the young shepherd boy met the challenge of 'the Philistine champion, Goliath', killed this giant who was 'over nine feet in height', and cut off his head. David then carried the head of Goliath in triumph to Jerusalem, and 'Abner took him and presented him to Saul with the Philistine's head still in his hand' (1 Sam. 17:4, 23–58). This is the scene depicted in this painting (**55**) by Nicolas Poussin (1549–1665) in the Dulwich Art Gallery, London.

55 *The Triumph of David, Nicolas Poussin, Dulwich Art Gallery, London*

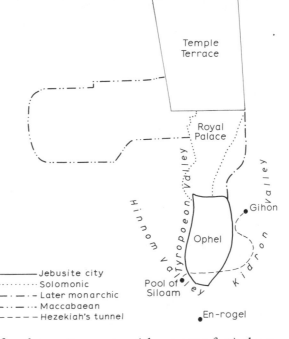

56 *Jerusalem in Old Testament times*

Temple
Terrace

Royal
Palace

Tyropoeon Valley

Hinnom Valley

Gihon

Ophel

Kidron Valley

———— Jebusite city
············ Solomonic
— · — · — Later monarchic
— · · — · · · Maccabaean
— — — — Hezekiah's tunnel

Pool of
Siloam

En-rogel

Jerusalem

The city of Jerusalem stands on a lofty plateau 830 metres (about 2723 feet) above sea level. In Old Testament times deep ravines almost surrounded the city: the Kidron Valley to the east and south; the Hinnom Valley, a continuation of the Kidron Valley, to the south and west; and the Tyropoeon Valley running north between the other two (map **56**). Building operations in modern times have greatly changed the contours of the city and its surroundings. In particular, the Tyropoeon Valley has been almost completely filled in, and only at its southern end is there any sign of it on the aerial photograph of the modern city (**57**).

The original city occupied only the hill called Ophel (map **56**), and excavations have shown that this area was inhabited from very early times, certainly before 3000 B.C. It was protected by a wall 8 metres (about 26 feet) thick, part of which

57 *Aerial view of Jerusalem from the south*

was discovered in 1927. This wall was so strong that the inhabitants could boast that their city needed only to be defended by 'the blind and the lame' (2 Sam. 5: 6).

It was this city of Ophel, sometimes called Jebus, that David's storm troops captured; according to one version of the Bible (A.V.) by climbing a 'gutter', according to another version (R.V.) by climbing 'the watercourse', but according to the New English Bible by each soldier using 'his grappling-iron' (2 Sam. 5: 8). The corresponding passage in the book of Chronicles says that the first man to kill a Jebusite was to become a commander in the army, and adds that 'the first man to go up was Joab' (1 Chron. 11: 6), but it does not mention either a gutter or grappling-irons. David's capture of a city protected by its natural defences as effectively as Jebus obviously was, called for military skill of outstanding quality, but we cannot now be sure of the details of this notable achievement. After it had been captured, David still further strengthened the city and made it his capital.

Solomon

Solomon was noisily anointed king in succession to David, his father. A trumpet was sounded, 'all the people shouted, "Long live King Solomon!"', and they 'escorted him home in procession, with great rejoicing and playing of pipes, so that the very earth split with the noise' (1 Kings 1: 39f.). Solomon inherited the territory won by David, and he exploited to the full its trading and commercial possibilities. He 'built a fleet of ships at Ezion-geber . . . on the shore of the Red Sea, in Edom' (1 Kings 9: 26), and these ships went as far as Ophir (probably south-west Arabia, or perhaps Somaliland) 'and brought back four hundred and twenty talents of gold' (1 Kings 9: 28). Solomon's 'fleet of merchantmen' returned to port 'once every three years . . . bringing gold and silver, ivory, apes and monkeys' (1 Kings 10: 22). Solomon also made full use of a caravan route which ran eastward from the Negeb to Arabia (map **59**), from which he received 'the tolls levied by the customs officers and profits on foreign trade, and the tribute of the kings of Arabia and the regional governors' (1 Kings 10: 15). This route was mainly used for the camel transport of precious spices and perfumes.

Solomon's activities may also have included the development of the copper-refining industry, although biblical evidence for this is absent. There are copper-bearing rocks on the eastern flank of the Arabah (map **3**) and elsewhere in the region, and it is thought that the ore may have been extensively mined in Solomon's day, as it probably was in earlier times. The photograph (**58**) shows some of these rocks near Ezion-geber. What appear to be the remains of furnaces, miners' huts, and slag heaps have been found. In searching for traces of Solomon's seaport at Ezion-geber (map **59**), Nelson Glueck found a large copper refinery of about

58 *Copper-bearing rocks near Ezion-geber*

the tenth century B.C., which he thought might have been built by Solomon. The buildings seem to be so arranged that the wind blowing down the Arabah (map **3**) might serve as the air blast to raise the temperature of the furnaces to the necessary intensity to refine the copper. Recently, however, it has been suggested that this is a misinterpretation of the evidence at Ezion-geber. The absence of large slag heaps and smelting implements left behind by the workmen, and the doubt expressed by meteorologists that the wind speed in the Arabah would be sufficient to bring the furnaces to the necessary temperature, have led some scholars to the conclusion that the buildings were not a copper refinery, but that they were part of a storage depot for goods waiting to be shipped from Ezion-geber. Further evidence is needed before a firm conclusion can be reached on this subject.

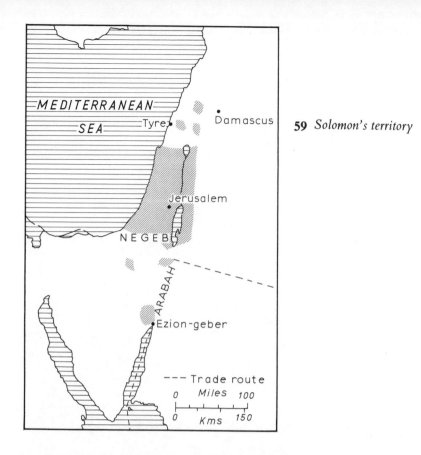

59 *Solomon's territory*

Solomon was not able to hold all the territory he inherited from David. The shaded areas on this map (**59**) show the probable extent of Solomon's kingdom at the end of his reign. As a result of trouble in Edom, where Hadad 'remained an adversary for Israel all through Solomon's reign' (1 Kings 11: 25), territory was almost certainly lost in the south, although Solomon probably held on to Ezion-geber and to a few other areas that were of special commercial value to him. He also had to face trouble in Syria, where 'Rezon . . . gathered men about him and became a captain of freebooters' (1 Kings 11: 23f.). As a result of this skirmishing in the north Solomon lost Damascus and control of the trade route associated with it.

In spite of these losses, Solomon's reign was in some respects the golden age in Israel's history. Apart from all else, the extent and the splendour of his building programme are sufficient to justify the description. He extended the Jebusite city northward (map **56**), and built 'the House of the Forest of Lebanon' (1 Kings 7: 2), a throne-room called 'the Hall of Judgement' (1 Kings 7: 7), and a palace for himself and his 'seven hundred wives, who were princesses, and three hundred concubines' (1 Kings 11: 3). His greatest achievement was, of course, the building of the temple at Jerusalem on a site to the north of the secular buildings, and this is dealt with in more detail below (pp. 158ff.).

The wisdom of Solomon

Solomon had a reputation for unusual wisdom. It is said that it 'surpassed that of all the men of the east and of all Egypt' (1 Kings 4: 30). A typical exhibition of Solomon's wise judgement was seen when 'two women who were prostitutes' brought a problem to him. Each of them had a baby, and one of the babies died. Both women claimed to be the mother of the living child. Solomon's solution of the problem was a simple one. He asked for a sword to be brought, and then gave the order; 'Cut the living child in two and give half to one and half to the other'. The two women soon made it clear which of them was the mother (1 Kings 3: 16–28). This picture (**60**) by the Flemish painter, Jacob Jordaens (1593–1678) in the Gallery del Prado, Madrid, dramatically portrays the scene.

60 *The Wisdom of Solomon, Jacob Jordaens, Gallery del Prado, Madrid*

Megiddo

The Plain of Esdraelon, or the Vale of Jezreel (map **1**, **61**), is the only significant break in the range of hills that runs the length of Palestine west of the Jordan Valley (diagram **2**). It is therefore the key to the whole area. Here two great trunk roads crossed in ancient times; one of them the commercial and military highway running north between Egypt and Syria, and thence to the Middle East, the other the east–west road from the Mediterranean coast that crossed the Jordan Valley to join the king's highway (map **31**). Megiddo guarded this crossing place, and to capture it was the aim of every military commander seeking to dominate the Near East. Solomon made it one of a chain of fortresses he built to defend his territory.

The tell at Megiddo has been systematically excavated (**61**), and twenty occupation levels have been found (**5**), the earliest of them probably reaching back to about 4000 B.C. Excavation of the lower layers resulted in the discovery of many important remains: including Canaanite and Israelite palaces containing priceless objects in bronze, gold, and carved ivory (**122**); and three Canaanite temples of about 3000 B.C. with the high places (pp. 152f.) and altars associated with them.

61 *Excavations at Megiddo, with Vale of Jezreel in the distance*

62 *Aerial view of the excavations at Megiddo*

This photograph of the excavated tell at Megiddo (**62**) was taken from a balloon 250 metres (about 820 feet) above the site. Solomon rebuilt and fortified the ancient city of Megiddo, perhaps making it one of 'the towns where he quartered his chariots and horses' (1 Kings 9: 19). A double gate of enormous strength, probably of Solomon's time, has been discovered at the northern edge of the mound (that is, near the bottom left-hand corner of this photograph). A ramp for chariots and other horse-drawn vehicles leads up to it, and huge wooden doors no doubt guarded this and the other entrances to the city. This gate and a fortress of the same period, recently discovered by Yigael Yadin, are constructed of carefully shaped and fitted stone blocks, the earliest appearance of this kind of building in Palestine. This development from the use of rough stones to the fitting together of shaped blocks of stone is almost certainly due to the influence of the Phoenician builders who were called in to assist in Solomon's building programme.

At Megiddo there is also to be seen the remains of a water system similar to the one at Jerusalem (pp. 124f. and map **56**), to supply water to the city in time of siege. It consists of a vertical shaft inside the city (the dark hole near the bottom right-hand corner of the photograph), and a horizontal tunnel leading from the spring outside the city to the bottom of this shaft. The entrance to the tunnel was hidden from the enemy by a wall and a mound of earth.

On the southern and eastern edges of the tell (that is, the top and the right-hand side of photograph **62**) extensive remains of stables have been found (**63**). A large courtyard with an enormous trough for watering the horses stood in front of the stable buildings. The floors of the stables were cobble-stoned, and the supporting pillars, with mangers between them, served also as tethering posts for the horses. Two stone mangers can be seen in position near the middle of the photograph. It has been estimated that there was accommodation at Megiddo for about 450 horses.

Until recently it was thought that these were stables for Solomon's cavalry, but further investigation suggests that they probably belong to the period of Ahab, some 70 years later than Solomon. Nevertheless, they may well be on the same site as Solomon's stables, rebuilt and perhaps enlarged by Ahab to meet the growing need for cavalry in face of the Assyrian attacks on Palestine (pp. 71ff.).

63 *Excavated stables at Megiddo*

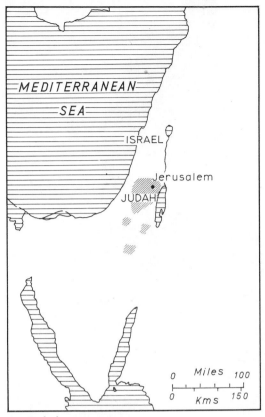

64 *Rehoboam's territory*

6. THE DIVIDED KINGDOMS

Rehoboam

Solomon died in about 922 B.C. and the rebellion that had smouldered during the closing years of his reign immediately burst into flame. Jeroboam, 'one of Solomon's courtiers . . . a man of great energy' (1 Kings 11 : 26–8), who had been the leader of the discontent, but had been compelled to escape to Egypt because Solomon sought to kill him, now returned and was crowned king 'over the whole of Israel' (1 Kings 12: 20), that is, the ten northern tribes (map **52**). Rehoboam had been to Shechem, expecting to be proclaimed king in succession to Solomon, but his reception was not enthusiastic, and he had to be content to rule over 'the tribe of Judah alone' (1 Kings 12: 20) and the neighbouring southern tribe of Benjamin. He probably also held a few pockets of territory further south, but the extent of them and the firmness with which they were held are unknown. The shaded areas on the map (**64**) suggest the probable extent of this remnant of the kingdom built up by Rehoboam's grandfather, partly lost by his father, and now reduced to its lowest ebb.

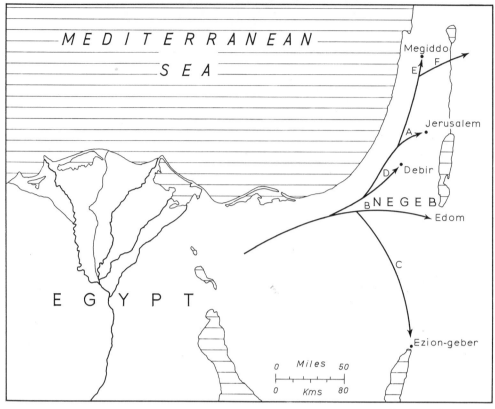

65 *Egyptian attacks*

Egyptian attacks (map **65**)

When, after Solomon's death, the kingdom was divided to create the rival king-doms of Israel in the north and Judah in the south (time-chart **11**), internal strife weakened the country and made it an easy prey to its enemies. Egypt, always ready to pounce on Palestine when she was strong enough to do so, took advantage of this situation and invaded Palestine from the south. The book of Kings speaks briefly of this invasion. It was 'in the fifth year of Rehoboam's reign' (that is, about 918 B.C.) that 'Shishak king of Egypt' attacked Jerusalem (A) and 'removed the treasures of the house of the LORD and of the royal palace, and seized every-thing, including all the shields of gold that Solomon had made' (1 Kings 14: 25–8).

Shishak's inscription on the south wall of the temple at Karnak (map **3**) gives a much embellished and probably exaggerated account of the campaign. It seems probable that the Egyptian army crossed the Negeb into Edom (B), and may have penetrated as far as Ezion-geber (C). There is archaeological evidence to show that Debir was destroyed at this time (D), and Megiddo is listed at Karnak as one of the defeated cities (E). Signs of the partial destruction of Megiddo by fire at about this time, and the discovery of a victory stele, point to Shishak's successful attack on the city. The army crossed the Vale of Jezreel (map **1**) and invaded the land east of the Jordan (F). Growing weakness at home compelled the Egyptians to abandon their gains in Palestine, but not before Judah had suffered a severe blow which banished her hopes of conquering Israel and recreating a united nation.

Assyrian attacks (map **66**)

The rise and fall of Assyrian power played an important part in international affairs during the Old Testament period. Even before the time of the patriarchs, Assyria was prominent in the politics of the Middle East, but her influence declined, reaching its lowest ebb during the reign of David (1000–961 B.C.). She gradually recovered her power. Nineveh, a 'blood-stained city . . . never empty of prey' (Nahum 3 : 1), was her capital, and during the reign of Omri (876–869 B.C.), Assyria was able to advance westward along the Fertile Crescent (map **26**) and to overcome the smaller states that lay in her way (A). When the Assyrian forces reached the Mediterranean coast they were able to compel the seaports, including Byblos and Tyre, to pay tribute. This expedition was little more than a military raid, but it foreshadowed the shape of things to come, and it should have warned Israel of the danger from the east to which she was exposed.

Near the beginning of the reign of Shalmaneser III of Assyria (859–824 B.C.), the army marched westward again (B) and the kings of the small Mediterranean states joined forces to meet the attack. The inscription describing Shalmaneser's

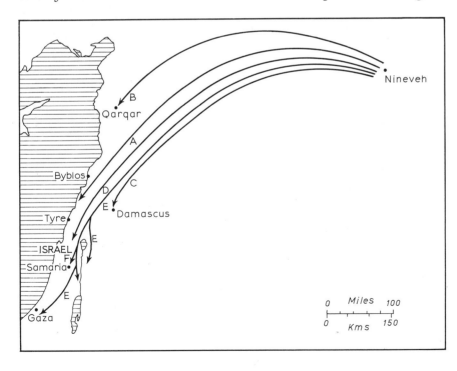

66 *Assyrian attacks*

military exploits (on a large stone slab found at Kurkh (map **4**) in 1861, now in the British Museum) says that Ahab, king of Israel, was a member of the coalition and that he contributed 200 chariots and 10,000 foot soldiers to meet the Assyrian invasion. The Bible does not mention this fact, does not name Shalmaneser, and does not record the battle that took place at Qarqar on the river Orontes in 853 B.C. when the Assyrian and the coalition forces clashed.

Shalmaneser's inscription claims a decisive victory for his army at Qarqar, and says that they killed 14,000 men and made a bridge across the Orontes with their corpses. This is probably an exaggeration of the kind often found in such inscriptions, and the truth seems to be that the coalition forces effectively stayed the Assyrian advance at least for the time being.

Damascus was attacked several times by the Assyrians during the reign of Shalmaneser III, most seriously in 841 B.C. when the city was besieged (C), but not conquered. During the same campaign the Assyrian army again reached the Mediterranean coast and took tribute from the seaports and from Jehu, king of Israel. This episode is described and illustrated on the Black Obelisk (pp. 85f.).

During the reign of Tiglath-pileser III (745–727 B.C.) the Assyrians made several serious military attacks on Syria, Tyre, Byblos, Damascus, and Israel (D). This king adopted for the first time on a large scale a new idea that was to be followed by his successors. Previous Assyrian kings had been content to take tribute from the states they conquered, but Tiglath-pileser III deported prisoners of war to Assyria or to other conquered territory and claimed the defeated states as part of his empire.

In 734 B.C. Tiglath-pileser marched westward (E), partly because the southern kingdom of Judah had called for his assistance against the attacks of Israel and Syria from the north (2 Kings 15: 37), of the Edomites from the east (2 Kings 16: 6; but see the footnote in the New English Bible), and of the Philistines from the south (2 Chron. 28: 18). But in conducting this campaign Tiglath-pileser was also following his own strong inclination, for Assyria was by this time intent on building up a massive empire. His army overran all Israel and the territory east of the Jordan, destroyed many cities, 'and deported the people to Assyria' (2 Kings 15: 29). The Philistine cities, including Gaza, were attacked, and a base was established to prevent help being sought from Egypt. Hoshea, king of Israel, surrendered and offered tribute to Assyria, thus saving Israel for the time being from complete destruction.

When Tiglath-pileser III was succeeded by his son, Shalmaneser V, Hoshea thought he saw an opportunity of regaining Israel's independence. He tried to make an alliance with 'the king of Egypt at So', and withheld 'the tribute which he had been paying year by year' to Assyria (2 Kings 17: 4). (Earlier versions of the English Bible say, 'So, king of Egypt', but no 'king' of that name can be identified; and the suggested amendment in the New English Bible may be more nearly correct.) Shalmaneser discovered Hoshea's disloyalty, and his army marched westward to punish it (F). 'He invaded the whole country and, reaching Samaria, besieged it for three years.' Samaria fell in 721 B.C. and Shalmaneser 'deported its people to Assyria' (2 Kings 17: 5f.). The northern kingdom of Israel was thus removed for ever from world history.

Samaria

It is perhaps not surprising that Samaria was able to resist the Assyrian attack for three years. This photograph (**67**) shows its position. Omri 'bought the hill of Samaria . . . for two talents of silver and built a city on it' (1 Kings 16: 24) to be his capital. The hill, seen in the background of the photograph, is only about 100 metres (328 feet) high, but it is surrounded by valleys on all sides, and thus is easy to defend. From its summit there is a clear view in all directions, as far as the Mediterranean coast to the west, and the approach of an enemy could be seen in time to prepare the defences of the city against attack. The sieges of Samaria were almost always long. It held out against a blockade by the Syrians until 'a donkey's head was sold for eighty shekels of silver, and a quarter of a kab of locust-beans for five shekels' (2 Kings 6: 25).

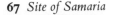

67 *Site of Samaria*

68 *Assyrian infantrymen*

Assyrian warfare

We are fortunate in having a great many illustrations of the methods of warfare used by the Assyrians during the period of the monarchy in Israel and Judah. Most of them were found by A. H. Layard in the palaces of the kings of Assyria at Nimrud (map **4**). They are in the form of huge alabaster panels and reliefs which decorated the walls of the palaces. Many of them are now in the Assyrian Gallery of the British Museum.

Assyrian infantrymen (**68**) were armed with short swords, bows and arrows, and slings. They were protected from enemy fire by tall wicker shields which rested on the ground and had curved tops to deflect arrows and sling-shot. Strong handles enabled attendants to hold the shields in position and to move them as required. The soldiers wore pointed hats with protective ear-pieces, long tunics and high boots.

69 *Assyrians attacking a walled city using a battering ram*

Battering rams were used to attack a walled city. This one (**69**) is a heavy unwieldy contraption on wheels, with a projection at the front like a boar's snout. The city depicted here has double walls, and two men are building a ramp of earth at the foot of the outer wall to enable the battering ram to be run up against the higher and weaker part of the wall. This scene is one of many on beaten bronze bands which were used to decorate the gates of the palace of Shalmaneser III at Nimrud.

The wheels of the battering ram in the previous illustration (**69**) are exposed to enemy fire and would easily be damaged. In this photograph (**70**) an improved type is shown. The wheels are protected by armour plate, two sharp-pointed

70 *Assyrians attacking a walled city using a battering ram*

ramrods are suspended by ropes and swung like a pendulum by soldiers inside the machine, which is covered with leather strengthened with metal discs. The ramrods have partly penetrated the wall, and archers, protected by wicker shields, bring up the rear. Three naked Israelites are brutally impaled on pointed stakes, perhaps in an attempt to frighten the defenders of the city into submission. Dead and wounded lie at the foot of the wall, and a man on the turret is either pleading with the attackers for mercy or offering the surrender of the city.

71 *Assyrian cavalrymen*

Assyrian cavalrymen (**71**) were armed with spears, bows and arrows (the soldier on the left is carrying his bow over his shoulder), and short swords (seen sticking out behind each of the soldiers). The men wear mail armour, but the horses seem to be unprotected. The horrors of chariot warfare are realistically represented in this photograph (**72**), in which the dead and wounded are being trampled by horses and run over by an Assyrian chariot.

72 *An Assyrian chariot*

73 *Evacuation of a city captured by the Assyrians*

When the Assyrians captured a city they took away the spoil and evacuated the inhabitants. This frieze (**73**) shows a double-walled city with turrets, evidently in a palm-growing area. The battering ram on the left has partly penetrated the wall. Women and children prisoners (men would be made to walk) are being taken away in carts drawn by oxen. Sheep and cattle are being driven out of the city by the victorious captors. Two scribes with writing materials in their hands are recording the spoil. In this scene (**74**) from the palace of Tiglath-pileser at Calah (map **4**), the city stands on a hill and has an outer wall with towers and a citadel (seen on the left at the top of the picture). The inscription names the city 'Astartu', probably Ashtaroth (map **1**), the headquarters of Og, king of Bashan (Deut. 1:4). Prisoners and sheep are being deported, following the capture of

74 *Spoil being taken from a city captured by the Assyrians*

75 *Assyrian soldiers returning from a victory*

the city. In this frieze (75) the soldiers of Sennacherib (705–681 B.C.) are bringing back to camp the heads of their enemies after a victory. Some of the soldiers carry round wicker shields, and a few prisoners are being brought in.

The kings themselves are sometimes depicted on the palace reliefs. This fine frieze (76) shows Tiglath-pileser III (745–727 B.C.), called 'Pul king of Assyria' in 2 Kings 15: 19, riding in his state chariot at the evacuation of Ashtaroth. He is standing beside the driver and an attendant holds a sunshade over him. The king is saluting some person or persons not shown here, but perhaps appearing

76 *Tiglath-pileser III in his state chariot*

on a part of the relief now lost. This relief (**77**) from the palace at Khorsabad, a few miles north of Nineveh (map **4**), shows Sargon, the conqueror of Samaria in 721 B.C., on the left. He holds a staff and is wearing his royal head-dress and robes, and is receiving one of his officials, probably his commander-in-chief.

77 *Sargon receiving an official*

Lachish

The city of Lachish occupied an important position on the lower western slopes of the Judaean hills, about 40 kilometres (25 miles) south-west of Jerusalem (map 1). It has a long history. It was fortified, perhaps as early as the eighteenth century B.C., by digging an artificial ditch round it and building a slope, made slippery with plaster to prevent attackers from scaling it. David built a palace there for a government official, and Rehoboam strengthened it, together with a number of other cities in Judah. Lachish was frequently attacked. For example, 'In the fourteenth year of the reign of Hezekiah, Sennacherib king of Assyria attacked and took all the fortified cities of Judah' (2 Kings 18: 13, but see footnote in New English Bible on 'fourteenth'). Lachish was almost certainly one of the 'fortified cities' mentioned in this text. On the north-west slope of the mound at Lachish a pit was found into which 1500 bodies had been thrown, probably during a clearing-up operation following Sennacherib's siege of the city. Three of the skulls found in this pit show signs of trepanning; that is, a surgical operation in which the skull is cut open to relieve pressure on the brain. Jehoiakim rebuilt the city, but it was heavily attacked by the Babylonians under Nebuchadnezzar and very thoroughly destroyed by fire in 589 B.C. The Lachish Letters (pp. 92f.) are dated from this period. After the return of the Jews from exile in Babylon, Nehemiah says that 'some of the men of Judah lived . . . in Lachish and its fields' (Neh. 11: 25, 30), but the city declined in importance and it was finally deserted in about 150 B.C.

Lachish has been extensively excavated. This photograph (**78**) shows the present appearance of Tell ed-Duweir, the site of ancient Lachish, looking toward the

78 *Tell ed-Duweir*

north-east corner of the tell. Lachish was one of the largest cities in Judah, and the flat summit of the mound covers about 18 acres (Megiddo has an area of about 13 acres, and Ophel about $11\frac{1}{2}$ acres). Rehoboam built a double wall round the city: the higher one 6 metres (nearly 20 feet) thick and of sun-dried mud bricks; the lower one, 15 metres (about 49 feet) down the slope, 4 metres (about 13 feet) thick and of stone and brick. In the illustration the appearance of the higher wall on top of the mound can easily be imagined, and the level of the lower wall can plainly be seen, especially on the right-hand side of the mound. A winding road near the middle of the photograph leads to the city gate.

79 *Reconstruction of the city of Lachish*

This drawing (**79**) by H. H. McWilliam shows these features and the probable appearance of the city in its heyday. Excavation has shown that both walls had alternate projections and recesses, with defensive towers at intervals. The battlements were probably of wood, for a large quantity of charcoal was found in the debris at the foot of the walls. The remains of soil ramps were also found near the outer wall, set up, no doubt, by the attackers of the city.

80 *Siege of Lachish*

These panels (**80** and **81**) are from Sennacherib's palace at Nineveh (map **4**), part of a large frieze depicting the siege of Lachish. They may be seen in the Assyrian Gallery of the British Museum. In the description that follows, the two photographs will be regarded as one picture.

Features already mentioned are to be seen: the double walls, the alternate projections and recesses in the walls, and the defensive towers. The battlements are manned by soldiers, some of whom are bowmen and others who are throwing stones and lighted firebrands at the attackers. The stones are formally represented as cubic shapes, but the burning ends of the falling firebrands are realistically depicted. Lengths of wood have been laid end to end in sets of three to give the infantry a foothold on the slippery slope of the city mound and to provide a track for the battering ram seen near the middle of the panel. This battering ram has four wheels; a long spear-like ramrod which is directed against the top, weaker part of the tall gate tower; and a crew of two, one a bowman, the other pouring

81 *Siege of Lachish*

water (which falls at an angle of 45 degrees!) from a long-handled ladle on a fire-
brand which has landed on the machine and might set alight its wooden or leather
parts.

The gate tower on the right has three small windows, and protecting shields
at the top. There are soldiers on its battlements, and citizens of Lachish are
escaping with some of their possessions through the city gate at the foot of the
tower. In the bottom right-hand corner of the picture three naked men of
Lachish are impaled on pointed wooden stakes. On the far left, spearmen are at
various levels on the earth and stone ramp. They carry large round wicker
shields. The bowmen on the highest level are pouring arrows into the city and are
themselves protected by a huge wicker shield. The contrast between the rough
texture of the ramp hurriedly built by the attackers and the smooth texture of
the plaster-covered slope made by the defenders in time of peace, is very skilfully
brought out by the artist.

The Moabite Stone

The kingdom of Moab (map **3**) developed alongside that of Israel, and Eglon, king of Moab, was one of the oppressors of Israel during the settlement period. In the period of the united monarchy, Moab was conquered by David; and in the period of the divided monarchy, Moab was forced to pay regular tribute to Israel. Following Ahab's death (according to the biblical account) Mesha, king of Moab, successfully rebelled and temporarily threw off the yoke of Israel, and it is the story of this rebellion that is told on the Moabite Stone (**82**). 'Omri, king of Israel' is named as the one who 'humbled Moab many days', and Moab's defeat at this time is attributed to the anger of Chemosh, their national god. Cities in Moab recaptured from Israel by Mesha are named, and a record of the king's building activity is included in the inscription.

The Moabite Stone was shown by an Arab sheikh to a German missionary at Dibon (map **I**), about 20 kilometres (12 miles) east of the Dead Sea, in 1868. It was 1·2 metres (about 46 inches) high, 0·6 metre (about 24 inches) wide, and about 26 centimetres (10 inches) thick. Rather than let it fall into the hands of the French or the German officials who were anxious to possess it, the Arabs made the stone hot on a fire, poured water over it to break it, and carried away the fragments. About two-thirds of it was eventually recovered and the jig-saw pieces were put together again. It was placed in the Louvre, Paris, in 1873.

The Moabite Stone is an inscription of very great historical importance, closely related both in style and content to the record in the Old Testament. It largely agrees with the biblical account of Mesha's revolt, allowing of course for the boastfulness that is almost always found in such inscriptions, but it places the revolt before the death of Ahab, whereas the Bible says the revolt broke out 'when Ahab died' (2 Kings 3: 5).

82 *The Moabite Stone*

83 *The Black Obelisk*

The Black Obelisk

In 1846 A. H. Layard, a young English excavator, found a black limestone pillar (**83**) at Nimrud, about 40 kilometres (25 miles) south of Nineveh (map **4**), where Shalmaneser III, king of Assyria (858–824 B.C.), had his palace. This Black Obelisk, as it is usually called, is 2 metres (about 6½ feet) high, and it originally stood in the public square at Nimrud. Following an adventurous journey over land and sea lasting nearly two years, the Black Obelisk reached the British Museum, where it is now to be seen. On it are carved five panels in bas-relief on each of its four sides, commemorating the events of the first thirty-one years of Shalmaneser's reign. The panels are intended to be read horizontally round the four sides of the pillar as a continuous frieze, and each of the five friezes represents a region from which Shalmaneser received tribute. Above each panel there is a description of the scene below it, and the stepped top of the obelisk above the panels and the base below them have longer inscriptions, totalling 210 lines altogether.

The second frieze from the top depicts the offering of tribute by Israel. The inscription names 'Jehu, son of Omri', and one of the panels (**84**) shows him

prostrate on hands and knees before the king of Assyria. Shalmaneser holds a bowl in his hand, and an attendant holds a sunshade over his head. Four Assyrians stand behind Jehu, and they are followed by a procession of thirteen Israelites carrying the tribute: 'silver, gold, a golden bowl, a golden vase ... golden tumblers, golden buckets, tin, a staff for a king'. Two of the four Assyrians can be seen behind Jehu on the second frieze from the top on the enlarged detail of the obelisk (**84**), and the other two Assyrians and eight of the thirteen Israelites can be seen on the same frieze on the general view of the obelisk (**83**). The Israelite porters on the Black Obelisk are all bearded, wear tasselled caps, and shoes with pointed up-turned toes. This representation of Jehu is the only known portrayal of an Israelite king.

An inscription on another monument says that Jehu offered tribute to Shalmaneser III in the year 841 B.C., but there is no mention of this event in the Bible. Jehu was not the 'son of Omri', as the inscription says, but he was, of course, his successor to the throne of Israel, and this may be the meaning of the phrase.

The Taylor Prism

Sennacherib, king of Assyria (705–681 B.C.), ordered accounts of his military exploits to be recorded on a number of hexagonal prisms. One of them, found at Nineveh (map **4**), is now in the British Museum (**85**). It is usually known as the Taylor Prism after the name of its first owner. It describes, among other things, the events which took place 'in the fourteenth year of the reign of Hezekiah' when 'Sennacherib king of Assyria attacked and took all the fortified cities of Judah' (2 Kings 18: 13). This prism was probably made in 691 B.C. and it contains the last of Sennacherib's records.

The biblical account of Sennacherib's siege of Jerusalem describes how the city was dramatically saved from destruction when 'the angel of the LORD went out and struck down a hundred and eighty-five thousand men in the Assyrian camp', so that 'when morning dawned, they all lay dead'. 'So', the writer adds, 'Sennacherib king of Assyria broke camp, went back to Nineveh and stayed there' (Isa. 37: 36f.). Sennacherib's own account of this episode, recorded on the Taylor Prism, presents a very different picture. The language is boastful, referring to Hezekiah 'like a caged bird . . . shut up in Jerusalem, his royal city'. It also describes Sennacherib's capture of 'forty-six strong walled cities' and the taking of many prisoners and much spoil: 'two hundred thousand, one hundred and fifty people, great and small, male and female, horses, mules, asses, camels, cattle and sheep without number', mentioning, in addition, the enormous annual tribute he claims to be able to extract from Hezekiah.

85 *The Taylor Prism*

Dog River inscriptions

These inscriptions (**86**) cut in the solid rock near the Dog River (p. 45) com–
memorate the military successes of the Assyrian armies. The figure of an Assyrian
king can be faintly seen on the slab on the left. Above these ancient inscriptions
a more modern plaque has been set up to record an allied victory at the end of
World War I.

86 *Dog River inscriptions*

87 *Isaiah, Michelangelo, Sistine Chapel*

Isaiah

Isaiah was called to be a prophet 'in the year of King Uzziah's death' (Isa. 6: 1), that is, 742 B.C., and he exerted a powerful influence in Jerusalem for nearly fifty years. This fresco (**87**) by Michelangelo (1475–1564) is part of the decoration of the Sistine Chapel, Rome (p. 24).

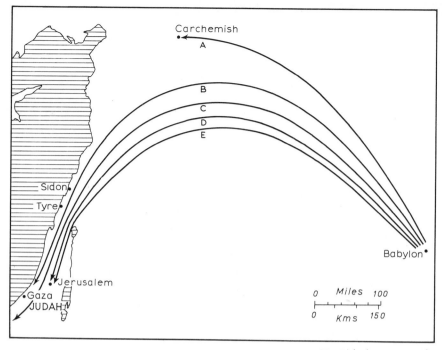

88 *Babylonian attacks*

7. EXILE AND RETURN

Babylonian attacks (map **88**)

Assyria came to the end of her military success when Nineveh, her capital, was captured by the Babylonians in 612 B.C., and when Harran was taken two years later. The book of Nahum powerfully portrays the attack on the 'blood-stained city' of Nineveh (Nahum 2: 1–13), describes the fall of the city (Nahum 3: 1–6), and gloats over the distress of the hated Assyrians (Nahum 3: 7–19).

Babylon now sought to expand her empire westward to the Mediterranean, as Assyria had done before her, but Egypt also hoped to take the Mediterranean states and include them in her empire. A clash was inevitable. An Egyptian army was encamped at Carchemish on the Euphrates, and the Babylonian army advanced on the city (A) and skirmishes took place. In 605 B.C. a pitched battle was fought in which 'Nebuchadrezzar king of Babylon' attacked and utterly defeated 'the army of Pharaoh Necho king of Egypt at Carchemish on the river Euphrates' (Jer. 46: 2).

In the next year the Babylonian army advanced again (B), this time as far south as 'the plain by the sea', where Philistia was 'despoiled', Tyre and Sidon 'destroyed to the last defender', Gaza 'shorn bare', and Ashkelon 'ruined' (Jer. 47: 4–7). Jehoiakim, king of Judah, deemed it wise to declare his allegiance to Nebuchadnezzar, so he 'became his vassal' (2 Kings 24: 1). Three years later Nebuchadnezzar again met the forces of Necho near the Egyptian frontier (C), and it seems probable that on this occasion the Babylonian army was defeated. This hitherto unknown battle is recorded in a fragment, one of four found in

1956, of the Babylonian Chronicle (pp. 91 f.). If it is an authentic record it makes plausible the decision of Jehoiakim that now was the moment to shake off the yoke of Nebuchadnezzar. For whatever reason, 'he broke with him and revolted' (2 Kings. 24: 1), and in the year that Jehoiakim died, the Babylonian army marched westward to punish Judah for her disloyalty (D). Jerusalem was besieged and 'Jehoiachin king of Judah, his mother, his courtiers, his officers, and his eunuchs, all surrendered to the king of Babylon' (2 Kings 24: 11f.). Nebuchadnezzar 'carried off all the treasures of the house of the LORD and of the royal palace . . . He carried the people of Jerusalem into exile . . .; only the weakest class of people were left' (2 Kings 24: 13f.).

Judah did not learn her lesson, and plots were hatched against Babylon, which eventually developed into open rebellion. When this became known to Nebuchadnezzar he 'advanced with all his army against Jerusalem, invested it and erected watch-towers against it on every side' (E), besieging the city until famine became severe 'and there was no food for the common people' (2 Kings 25: 1–3). Jerusalem held out heroically, but the walls were eventually pierced and a month later 'Nebuzaradan, captain of the king's bodyguard, came to Jerusalem and set fire to the house of the LORD and the royal palace; all the houses in the city . . . were burnt down'. In 586 B.C. the walls of the city were destroyed and 'the rest of the people left in the city' were deported to Babylon. Only 'the weakest class of people' were left behind 'to be vine-dressers and labourers' (2 Kings 25: 8–12). The southern kingdom of Judah thus disappeared from the political scene.

The Babylonian Chronicle

The Assyrian period is recorded so fully and illustrated so magnificently that our detailed knowledge of the ninth and eighth centuries B.C. is probably greater than that of any other period in biblical history. Unfortunately, the same cannot be said of the Babylonian period, which succeeded the Assyrian. Happily, however, the few sources of information we possess are of the highest quality and almost free from the boastful tone and the gross exaggeration that are characteristic of the Assyrian inscriptions.

In 1887 there appeared a translation of some cuneiform writing on a number of clay tablets that had been found in Babylon (map **4**). Other translations followed in 1923 and 1956, and it became apparent that here was a detailed, mainly contemporary, and almost certainly reliable, account of the Assyrian and Babylonian periods of biblical history. This collection of tablets is now known as the Babylonian Chronicle, and it is thought to have been compiled in the sixth century B.C. The fall of Nineveh, the ancient capital of Assyria, in 612 B.C., the

89 *Part of the Babylonian Chronicle*

battle of Carchemish in 605 B.C., the capture of Jerusalem in 597 B.C., the fall of Babylon and the rise of Cyrus to power in the east are all described in some detail, largely confirming and remarkably supplementing the biblical record of this period of history. The tablets are now in the British Museum.

The tablet shown here (**89**) is one of the four translated in 1956, the one on which is described the battle of Carchemish and the capture of Jerusalem 'in the seventh year . . . and on the second day of the month of Adar'. 'In the seventh year' means the seventh year of Nebuchadnezzar's reign; that is, 698/7 B.C. According to this information, Jerusalem fell on 16 March 597 B.C.

The Lachish Letters

Lachish was one of the cities destroyed by burning when Nebuchadnezzar overran Judah (pp. 90f.). Among the ashes in a small guard room near the outer gate of the city, J. L. Starkey, a British archaeologist, found eighteen pieces of broken pottery in 1935, and three more in 1938, on which short messages had been written in ink. These fragments are known today as the Lachish Letters. On some of them the Hebrew writing is no longer legible, the intense heat of the fire having almost obliterated the words. On the other fragments about one hundred lines in all can be read fairly easily. Some of the Lachish Letters are in the Palestine Archaeological Museum, Jerusalem, and others are in the British Museum. They date from the time of the prophet Jeremiah.

Most of the letters were sent to Yaosh, who may have been the officer in command of Lachish, probably by Hoshaiah, who was in charge of a smaller outpost further north. Yaosh was evidently a superior officer, for Hoshaiah

90 *Two sides of a letter from Lachish*

addresses him as 'my lord Yaosh'. The letters give us a first-hand impression of the political and military situation in Judah immediately before the destruction of Jerusalem in 586 B.C., and the tone of them reflects the worries and anxieties of men living in a small country under attack by a great power.

Letter IV, both sides of which are illustrated here (**90**), concludes by saying, '... and my lord will know that we are watching for the signals of Lachish ... for we cannot see Azekah'. This seems to suggest that fire or smoke signals were used in time of war, but the reason for not being able to see the signals from Azekah (if that is what the phrase means) is not certain. Azekah and Lachish, 'the only fortified cities left in Judah' at the time (Jer. 34: 7), were about 20 kilometres (12 miles) apart (map **1**). This distance, or a hill between the two places, or the climatic conditions may account for the absence of signals. Azekah may even have fallen into the hands of the Babylonians by the time this letter was written.

Jeremiah

Jeremiah was born about 650 B.C., and he was 'a prophet to the nations' during the period of Judah's decline and fall. This representation of him (**91**) is by Claes Sluter (*ca.* 1350–1406), an important Dutch master who left Holland at the invitation of Philip the Bold to help decorate the Carthusian monastery at Dijon. The figure of Jeremiah is one of several on the Moses Fountain, which was constructed in 1399 and stands in the courtyard of the monastery.

91 *Jeremiah, Claes Sluter, Dijon*

The Cyrus Cylinder

During extensive excavations in Babylon (map **4**), carried out by Hormuzd Rassam between 1879 and 1882, this clay, barrel-shaped inscription (**92**) was found. The writing is cuneiform and it is read by rotating the cylinder. Scholars think it was written about 536 B.C. It is known as the Cyrus Cylinder and it is to be seen in the British Museum.

92 *The Cyrus Cylinder*

In 539 B.C. Cyrus the Mede overthrew the Babylonian empire and united the Medes and the Babylonians to form the Persian empire, of which he then became king. The words inscribed on the cylinder give Cyrus' own account of his conquest of Babylon, saying that 'without fighting or battle . . . he averted hardship to Babylon'. Modesty is thrown to the wind, and Cyrus boasts, 'I am Cyrus, king of the world, great king, mighty king, king of Babylon', and adds much more in the same strain. An enlightened ruler, he quickly established a policy of toleration toward those holding different opinions from his own. The Assyrian and Babylonian practice had been to deport conquered peoples. Cyrus reversed this procedure and ordered the return of all prisoners of war to their own countries. Writing of the areas from which the prisoners came, he says, 'I gathered together all their inhabitants and restored them to their dwellings.' The Jews captured when Jerusalem fell were among those released. They were allowed to return to Palestine after their long exile 'by the rivers of Babylon' (Ps. 137: 1), and were encouraged to 'rebuild the house of the LORD in Jerusalem' (Ezra 1: 5).

The Bible also records these events. It is said that 'Cyrus king of Persia' made this declaration: 'To every man of his people now among you I say, the LORD his God be with him, and let him go up' (2 Chron. 36: 23). Ezra amplifies this brief statement attributed to Cyrus, adding that it was the LORD who 'stirred up the heart of Cyrus king of Persia' to liberate the prisoners, and that the proclamation of liberty was made throughout the kingdom, 'both by word of mouth and in writing' (Ezra 1: 1). There is no need to assume that these words were the actual ones used by Cyrus. It seems obvious that they are a Jewish version of what the king actually said. The religious overtones were probably added for purposes of propaganda; perhaps to encourage the Jews to begin immediately and enthusiastically the work of rebuilding the temple when they arrived back in Jerusalem.

Babylon

The city of Babylon (map **4**) was surrounded by an enormous wall, about 18 kilometres (11 miles) long and 26 metres (85 feet) thick. Part of the wall as it appears today, still about 18 metres (59 feet) high, is shown here (**93**). The wall was pierced by eight entrances, each having a gate named after a Babylonian god. The Ishtar Gate, which guarded an entrance on the north side of the city, can be seen between square towers to the right of the picture. An inscription says that Nebuchadnezzar built the Ishtar Gate in honour of Marduk. This fine reconstruction of it (**94**) is in the Staatliche Museum, Berlin.

Animal reliefs are characteristic of the Babylonian architecture of the period, and it is estimated that there were about 575 animals, bulls and dragons in alternate rows, on the walls and gates of Babylon (**93, 94**). They are each about one metre (slightly more than one yard) high and they are made of glazed tile. A processional street ran from the Ishtar Gate to the centre of the city. Nebuchadnezzar was mainly responsible for its construction. This thoroughfare, 23 metres (about 75 feet) wide, was flanked by walls of blue enamelled bricks on which

94 *Reconstruction of the Ishtar Gate*

93 *The walls of Babylon*

95 *Lion relief from the walls of Babylon*

stood in relief about 120 lions, white with yellow manes and yellow with red manes, each about two metres (6½ feet) high. The one with formal decoration added (95) is now in the Louvre, Paris, and the other (96) is in the Kunst Historisches Museum, Vienna.

96 *Lion relief from the walls of Babylon*

97 *The inscription at Behistun*

The inscription at Behistun

Few men can have taken more trouble to preserve a record of their exploits than
Darius I, king of Persia (521–486 B.C.). He caused a bas-relief and an inscription
in three languages to be carved at Behistun (map **4**) on a rock-face 115 metres
(about 377 feet) above the caravan route between Baghdad and Tehran (**97**).
The relief shows Darius and two attendants, with nine rebel prisoners roped

98 *Head of Darius at Behistun*

together in front of him. The figure of Darius is about three metres (nearly ten feet) high. This near view of the head of Darius on the relief (**98**) depicts him with a curled beard and moustache.

When the carving was completed, the workmen smoothed off the rock-face below it to make the last 33 metres (108 feet) unclimbable without the aid of ropes and ladders. H. C. Rawlinson, an English officer stationed near Behistun and a student of Oriental languages, made the first successful attempt between 1835 and 1847 to copy the inscription. He risked his life by standing on the top rung of a ladder to read the highest row of writing. In 1948 G. G. Cameron made a fresh study of the inscription, and the photographs reproduced here are some of those he took at that time.

The inscriptions, which are not easy to see in this photograph (**97**), are to the right and below the relief. One version of the inscription, that below the relief, is in Persian, and the other two versions are translations of it; one of them in cuneiform (p. 30). It was this trilingual engraving that gave scholars the key that unlocked the mystery of cuneiform writing and enabled it to be read for the first time. Translations of this boastful account of the victories of Darius have been found in other parts of the world; one of them at Elephantine among the Aramaic documents associated with the Jewish colony in Egypt (p. 100).

99 *A papyrus marriage document from Elephantine*

Elephantine Papyri

From time to time during the early years of this century, sheets of papyrus with Aramaic writing on them were found in Egypt. Originally these sheets had been rolled, flattened tightly, tied, and sealed, and some of them were still in this form when they were found. Others had been opened and could easily be read. This photograph (**99**) shows the state of one of these documents when it was received at the Brooklyn Museum, USA, where the Elephantine Papyri are now to be seen. An unskilled attempt to open it by cutting the folds and bends had brought it to this condition. Worse still, some of the cut pieces had been lost; but happily they were eventually found among the fragments of several other documents. It took nine months of expert craftsmanship to open and assemble the pieces of this sheet. It turned out to be a most elaborate Aramaic marriage agreement, written on 2 October 420 B.C. The bride's possessions, including her cosmetics, are listed in great detail – in case of divorce, when she would be allowed to take them away with her.

Aramaic was the language spoken by the people of northern Syria and north-west Mesopotamia, but it gradually spread to other parts of the Near East. It was evidently understood by the Hebrews at the time of the Assyrian siege of Jerusalem in 701 B.C. (p. 87), for during the negotiations one of them said to Sennacherib's chief officer, 'Please speak to us in Aramaic, for we understand it' (2 Kings 18: 26). One verse of Jeremiah (10: 11) and parts of Daniel (2: 4 – 7: 28) and Ezra (4: 8 – 6: 18) were written in Aramaic.

These Aramaic papyri found in Egypt came originally from Elephantine (map **3**), an island in the Nile opposite Aswan, where a colony of Jewish soldiers and traders lived in the fifth century B.C. The original colonists may have fled there when Jerusalem was destroyed in 586 B.C. (p. 91). If they did, it was against the advice of Jeremiah, who said to them, 'Do not go to Egypt', and predicted that if they went they would 'die by sword, by famine, and by pestilence' (Jer. 42: 19–22). Eventually, Jeremiah himself was forcibly removed to Egypt, along with 'the remnant of Judah', and this pathetic little band, 'disobeying the LORD', settled at Tahpanhes (map **3**) on the Nile delta (Jer. 43: 5–7).

The colonists at Elephantine built a temple to Yahu, perhaps a form of the name Yahweh, but it was destroyed by the Egyptians in about 410 B.C. This letter (**100**), written in November 407 B.C., is from the Jewish priests at Elephantine and is addressed to Bagoas, the Persian governor of Judah. The writers complain that they have previously written to the high priest of Jerusalem, but have received no reply. They are now asking for an assurance to present to the Egyptian officials that theirs is genuine Jewish worship. This assurance may have been withheld because the Jews at Elephantine worshipped Yahweh side by side with a number of other gods and goddesses. In any case, sacrifices offered elsewhere than at Jerusalem were contrary to the law which says, 'See that you do not offer your whole-offerings in any place at random' (Deut. 12: 13). It is clear that the Jews at Elephantine had moved away from the strict orthodoxy that was observed in Jerusalem in the days of Ezra and Nehemiah. The difficulty of determining the dates of the return of Ezra and of Nehemiah to Jerusalem from exile in Babylon is mentioned elsewhere (pp. 23 f.). Study of the Elephantine papyri throws light on this problem.

Ezra left Babylon 'in the seventh year of King Artaxerxes' (Ezra 7: 7–9), and Nehemiah left 'in the twentieth year of King Artaxerxes' (Neh. 2: 1–6), but it is

100 *A papyrus letter from Elephantine*

not clear from these texts whether the king referred to is Artaxerxes I (464–424 B.C.) or Artaxerxes II (404–358 B.C.). When Nehemiah began to rebuild the walls of Jerusalem he was helped by 'Eliashib the high priest and his fellow priests' (Neh. 3: 1), but one of the Elephantine letters tells us that Eliashib's 'grandson' (Ezra 10: 6; N.E.B. footnote, 'son') was high priest when this letter was written in 408 B.C. Furthermore, another letter written in 408 B.C. and sent from Elephantine to Jerusalem mentions the request made to the sons of Sanballat asking for help in rebuilding the temple at Elephantine, Sanballat by that time presumably being too old to deal with the matter. In his earlier days Sanballat was a contemporary of Nehemiah. It is therefore impossible to believe that Nehemiah came to Jerusalem as late as the reign of Artaxerxes II, and it seems highly probable that he came in the twentieth year of the reign of Artaxerxes I; that is, 444 B.C.

There is no agreement among scholars about the date of the return of Ezra, and suggested dates include 458 B.C., 428 B.C., and 398 B.C.

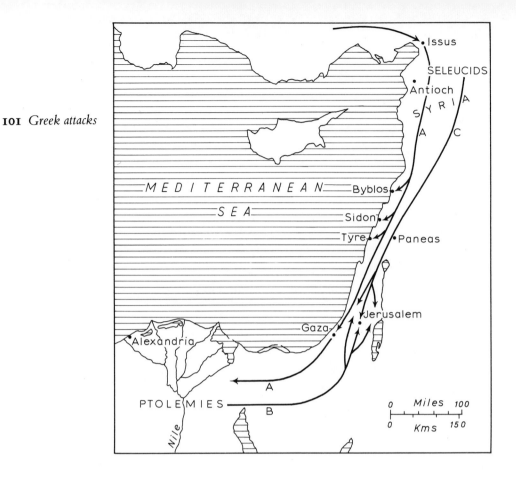

101 *Greek attacks*

8. THE HELLENISTIC PERIOD

Greek attacks (map 101)

Philip of Macedon was assassinated in 336 B.C., and his son Alexander, then only twenty years old, succeeded him. With the rapid rise to power of Alexander, known later as Alexander the Great (336–323 B.C.), the Persian empire declined and fell. Alexander, who had been a favourite pupil of Aristotle, at the time of his death at the age of thirty-three had conquered the world, having 'in the course of many campaigns . . . captured fortified towns, slaughtered kings, traversed the earth to its remotest bounds, and plundered innumerable nations' (1 Macc. 1: 2f.). The author of the book of Daniel describes this remarkable conquest like this: 'Suddenly a he-goat came from the west skimming over the whole earth without touching the ground' (Dan. 8: 5). This statue of Alexander the Great (102) is in the Capitoline Museum, Rome. It shows the young king wearing highly decorative armour, helmet and boots.

When Alexander had overcome the opposition of the Persian army under Darius III, he overran Asia Minor, but Darius rallied his forces and the Greeks and the Persians clashed when Alexander tried to enter Syria. A battle took place at Issus in 333 B.C. and Alexander's victorious army poured through the Cilician Gate, a narrow mountain pass leading into Syria. The Greeks now marched south along the coastal plain of Palestine toward Egypt (A). The seaports of Phoenicia, Byblos, Sidon, and others, were easily captured, but Tyre endured a seven months' siege before admitting defeat. Alexander met no other serious opposition until he reached Gaza, which was taken only after a two months' siege. In 332 B.C. Alexander entered Egypt, where he was welcomed as a liberator from the hated Persians and hailed as a successor to the Pharaohs. He sacrificed to Apis, the sacred bull, and established a new city on the Nile delta, one of the many to be called Alexandria in his honour, and soon to become the cultural capital of the world and the home of many immigrant Jews.

Alexander died during a campaign in Babylon, but when he fell ill, 'knowing that he was dying, he summoned his generals, nobles who had been brought up with him from childhood, and divided his empire among them' (1 Macc. 1: 5f.). When Alexander died, 'his generals . . . were all crowned as kings' (1 Macc. 1: 8f.). Two only of these rival kings are of interest to us here: Ptolemy I who ruled over Egypt, and Seleucus I who eventually ruled over Syria. Palestine, lying between the two, was a bone of contention for more than a century. Ptolemy,

102 *Statue of Alexander the Great, Capitoline Museum, Rome*

like many Egyptian rulers before and after him, was anxious to possess Palestine, and he conducted a number of campaigns in the attempt to gain his objective (B). He took it and lost it at least twice, but at the decisive battle of Ipsus in Phrygia in 301 B.C. Ptolemy gained control of Palestine and it remained in the hands of his successors, the Ptolemies, during most of the third century B.C.

103 *Towers in the walls of Samaria*

These magnificent towers are built in the repaired and strengthened walls of Samaria (**103**). They are Greek rather than Palestinian in architectural style, and they point to the Greek occupation of the city during the early Hellenistic period. The discovery in 1962 of a large number of legal and administrative documents written in Samaria (the Samaria papyri), a vast amount of pottery, and more than 200 skeletons in a cave in a desolate region north of Jericho, has shed much light on the history of Samaria at this time.

The successors of Seleucus, the Seleucids, tried to take Palestine from the Ptolemies, but they were unsuccessful until Antiochus III, known as Antiochus the Great, came to the throne. He was a vigorous ruler and after a series of campaigns in Palestine (C), which were sometimes successful, sometimes a failure, he finally in 198 B.C. won the battle of Paneas (map **101**) and Palestine passed from the Ptolemies into the hands of the Seleucids. The Jews seem to have been generously treated by Antiochus III, but this policy was violently reversed during the reign of his son, 'that wicked man, Antiochus Epiphanes' (1 Macc. 1: 10), regarded by Jews as one of the darkest periods in their long history of persecution and degradation.

The records of these events are scanty and not always reliable, and the diagrammatic representations on the map (**101**) of the campaigns must be taken as suggestive rather than strictly accurate.

The Maccabaean kingdom

The Jews were subjected to powerful Greek influences from the time of Alexander the Great until the revolt of 167 B.C. (p. 106), and some of them willingly absorbed the culture with which they were surrounded. They 'built a sports-stadium in the gentile style in Jerusalem. They removed their marks of circumcision and repudiated the holy covenant. They intermarried with Gentiles, and abandoned themselves to evil ways' (1 Macc. 1: 14f.). Greek became the language commonly spoken not only in Palestine but in the whole of the civilized world.

When Antiochus Epiphanes came to the throne in 175 B.C. he increased the pressure of Hellenism and interfered with Jewish religious life in a way no king before him had ever done. In 169 B.C. he 'entered the temple and carried off the golden altar, the lamp-stand with all its equipment, the table for the Bread of the Presence, the sacred cups and bowls, the golden censers, the curtain, and the crowns' (1 Macc. 1: 21f.). He gave orders that all copies of the law were to be destroyed, and that sacrifices, sabbath observance, festival celebrations, and circumcision were to be discontinued. 'The penalty for disobedience was death' (1 Macc. 1: 50). An altar to Zeus was erected in the temple in December 167 B.C. and a pig was sacrificed on it. This pagan altar is called 'the abomination of desolation' (Dan. 12: 11, 1 Macc. 1: 54, Mark 13: 14).

Not all the Jews accepted Hellenism; some resisted it fiercely. Those who opposed Antiochus were cruelly persecuted and horribly tortured, and many of

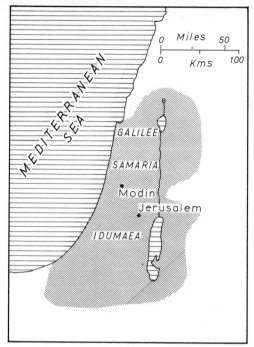

104 *The Maccabaean kingdom*

them died heroically rather than give up their obedience to the law. Eventually the situation became intolerable, and revolution broke out against the Greek oppression. At Modin (map **104**), a village about 27 kilometres (17 miles) north-west of Jerusalem in the Judaean hills, the aged Mattathias and his five sons launched an attack against the Seleucids in 167 B.C. Mattathias died a few months later and Judas, his third son, took on the leadership of the revolution. He was nicknamed Maccabee, and the movement is usually named after him and called the Maccabaean Revolt. From the start Judas Maccabaeus was victorious in battle, and in 164 B.C. Jerusalem was recaptured from the Greeks and the temple was cleansed of its pagan defilement. The joyous festival of Hanukkah is still kept annually by orthodox Jews in celebration of this happy event (p. 175).

Successful campaigns were conducted by Judas and his brothers, Jonathan and Simon, and their successors, in which territory was recovered and a Maccabaean kingdom was established. Jonathan built a fortress on the flat summit of a rocky plateau which he named Masada (**105**). It stands near the desolate west shore of the Dead Sea (map **1**), and it was here that Herod built his palace-fortress in New Testament times. Excavations at Masada have discovered the remains of the fortress and a number of important scrolls containing passages from biblical and other ancient books.

In 160 B.C. Judas was killed in battle. He was succeeded in turn by his brothers Jonathan and Simon, both of whom 'assumed the vestments of the high priest' (1 Macc. 10: 21) and were at the same time rulers of the people. Judas gained religious independence for the Jews, and under Simon complete political independence was eventually attained. John Hyrcanus, Simon's third surviving son, next became high priest and ruler in 134 B.C., and the struggle against the Seleucids was brought to an end as the result of a series of campaigns. Soon after this the nationalist hopes of the Jews reached their greatest height, and the shaded area on the map (**104**) shows the approximate extent of the Maccabaean kingdom at this time.

105 *Masada*

Hellenistic architecture

Edfu is a small Egyptian town, once a regional capital, on the west bank of the Nile about 100 kilometres (62 miles) south of Karnak (map **3**). In 1860 the debris covering a building was removed and there was disclosed one of the most perfectly preserved monuments of ancient times: the temple of the god Horus. The work of the Ptolemies (pp. 103f.), it was begun by Ptolemy III in 237 B.C. and not completed until 57 B.C. A small temple (**106**) was put up by Ptolemy IV; the forecourt and the great solid pylons (**107**) are the work of Ptolemy VIII and Ptolemy IX; and another temple (seen in the left foreground of **107**, and in greater detail in **108**) was built by Ptolemy VI and Ptolemy VII.

Horus, the god originally worshipped in the temple at Edfu, was a sun-god, and he is sometimes represented by a winged sun-disc (see **175**). At other times Horus seems to have been represented by a falcon, and two falcon images can be seen guarding the entrance to the great pylon (**107**), and another, and perhaps the remains of a second, are seen standing at the entrance to the small temple (**106**).

The influence of Hellenism is clearly seen in the architecture of Edfu. The huge wall spaces are filled with bas-reliefs of the traditional kind, depicting kings slaying their enemies, but the decoration on the columns is in the Greek style. Notice, for example, the elaborate flower and foliage carvings on the capitals at the top of the columns. The temple at Edfu is an illustration of the kind of religion and the kind of culture which some Jews enthusiastically embraced during the Hellenistic period, and which other Jews valiantly rejected, many of them to the point of death (pp. 105f.).

106 *Temple at Edfu*

107 *The great pylons at Edfu*

108 *Temple of Horus at Edfu*

109 *Temple of Bacchus at Baalbek*

110 *Temple of Jupiter at Baalbek*

III *Colonnade at Jerash*

The Romans were better engineers than architects, and in many of their buildings they were content to copy the Greek style of decoration, especially in the use of flower and foliage carving on the capitals of supporting columns. Thus the temples of Bacchus and Jupiter (**109** and **110**) at Baalbek (map **3**), and the colonnade (**III**) at Jerash (map **1**), although of the Roman period, illustrate very well the architectural characteristics of the Hellenistic period, which made such a powerful impact on the Jews at this time.

Petra

The ancient city of Petra stands in ruins on a rocky height of reddish sandstone about 80 kilometres (50 miles) south of the Dead Sea (map **3**). It has been described as 'a rose-red city half as old as time' (*Petra*, J. W. Burgon. In fact, there has been a city settlement here only from about 300 B.C.). Petra played a part in ancient history and it stood on one of the most important trade routes in biblical times, linking Ezion-geber with Damascus (map **31**). It is surprising therefore that there is no direct reference to it in the Bible.

Archaeological evidence shows that Petra was a human habitation from earliest times, with people living in cave dwellings, and that in the thirteenth century B.C. the Edomites made it their capital. Jeremiah may be referring to this when he says of the Edomites that they 'haunt the crannies among the rocks' and have built their nest 'high as a vulture' (Jer. 49: 16). In the late fourth century and on into the third century B.C. the Nabataeans, Arab traders and merchants controlling a vast commercial empire, made Petra their central stronghold. Petra played a not unimportant part in the Maccabaean struggle during the first century B.C.

The aerial view of Petra (**112**) shows the almost inaccessible site of the city. At the foot of the cliff can be seen some of the many royal tombs cut in the solid

112 *Aerial view of Petra*

rock and built in the Hellenistic style. The near view (**113**) brings out the architectural details in one of these tombs. Several unfinished tombs make it clear that the workmen cut the buildings from the top downward. A place of sacrifice at Petra will be described later (p. 152).

113 *Royal tombs at Petra*

Daniel

A casual reading of the book of Daniel would give the impression that it is describing incidents that occurred in the sixth century B.C. 'Jehoiakim king of Judah' and 'Nebuchadnezzar king of Babylon' are mentioned in the opening verse of the book, and the first part of the story takes place in Nebuchadnezzar's court and is about four young Jewish exiles who have been carried away to Babylon. Closer study of the book shows, however, that it belongs to the Maccabaean period, that the author probably used a number of earlier stories with a Babylonian background, and that it was written to encourage the Jews to stand firm against the bitter persecution of Antiochus Epiphanes in the second century B.C. (pp. 105f.).

114 *Daniel in the Lion's Den, B. Riviere, Walker Art Gallery, Liverpool*

The well-known story of Daniel in the lions' pit is intended to teach the tortured Jews that, in spite of all appearances, their God is 'a saviour, a deliverer, a worker of signs and wonders in heaven and on earth' (Dan. 6: 27), and that as God kept Daniel from harm in his time of great danger, so he will keep the Jews in theirs. This picture (**114**) by B. Riviere (1840–1920) in the Walker Art Gallery, Liverpool, shows Daniel with his hands bound behind his back confronting the angry lions calmly and confidently. When Daniel was brought out of the pit 'no trace of injury was found on him, because he had put his faith in his God' (Dan. 6: 23). The human bones on the floor of the pit show, however, that the lions had normal appetites, and when 'Daniel's accusers were brought and thrown into the lions' pit with their wives and children' this was speedily confirmed, for 'before they reached the floor of the pit the lions were upon them and crunched them up, bones and all' (Dan. 6: 24).

This painting (**115**) by J. R. Herbert (1810–90) in the Harris Art Gallery, Preston, Lancashire, shows Nebuchadnezzar surrounded by followers in his court in Babylon, with the youthful Daniel bringing down the judgement of God upon him. Nebuchadnezzar has had a dream about 'a tree of great height at the centre of the earth' which 'grew and became strong, reaching with its top to the sky and visible to earth's farthest bounds' (Dan: 4: 10f.). Five of Nebuchadnezzar's wise men are seen in the picture seated on either side of Daniel. None of them is able

115 *The Judgement of Daniel, J. R. Herbert, Harris Art Gallery, Preston*

to interpret the king's dream, but Daniel understands it perfectly. The mighty tree stands for Nebuchadnezzar himself in all his earthly power and glory. The king has a second dream, this time about 'a Watcher, a Holy One coming down from heaven' to 'hew down the tree, lop off the branches, strip away the foliage, scatter the fruit' (Dan. 4: 13f.). Daniel interpreted this to mean that judgement would come upon Nebuchadnezzar because he had set himself up as God's equal.

In this story Nebuchadnezzar is Antiochus Epiphanes in flimsy disguise. 'Epiphanes' was a nickname given to Antiochus IV because of his claim to god-like authority. It means 'god manifest', and some of the coinage of the period shows Antiochus identified with Zeus (p. 135). The author of this episode in the book of Daniel assures the Jews now under the yoke of Antiochus that God is about to destroy the tyrant and that the hour of their deliverance is near.

Tobit

The book of Tobit is in the Apocrypha (p. 145). It tells a pious tale that sounds like a folk-story. The unknown author has brought together material from several different sources: Egyptian, Babylonian, and Persian fables, and perhaps the book of Genesis. The main theme of the story is that great blessing comes to those who give alms to the needy, but there are subsidiary themes woven round the main one.

An account is first given of Tobit's righteousness, his generosity and his many good works. In spite of all this, much trouble has come his way: all his possessions have been forcibly taken from him, he is mocked by his neighbours, he suspects that his wife is a thief, and he has gone blind. He longs for death. Then he remembers 'the silver that he had deposited with Gabael at Rages in Media' (Tobit 4: 1), and he commands his son, Tobias, to find a worthy companion to go with him to recover the money. Tobias chooses Raphael, 'not knowing he was an angel of God' (Tobit 5: 5). They go off together and Tobias takes his pet dog with him.

When they reached the river Tigris 'a huge fish leapt out of the water and tried to swallow the boy's foot' (Tobit 6: 2). The angel told Tobias to cut open the fish 'and take out its gall, heart, and liver', but to 'throw the guts away' (Tobit 6: 4). They then 'cooked and ate part of the fish' and salted and kept the rest (Tobit 6: 5). This painting (**116**) by an artist of the Tuscan School of the fifteenth century, in the National Gallery, London, depicts the scene, but it is difficult to reconcile some of the details with the story as it appears in the book of Tobit. The angel, Tobias, and the little dog are easy to identify, but if Raphael had the appearance shown in this painting it is impossible to believe that Tobias did not recognize that he was an angel. Tobias has in his left hand the fish and the 'note of hand' (Tobit 5: 3) which will guarantee the return of Tobit's money, but the fish has certainly not had its gall, heart, and liver taken out, still less has it been roasted and eaten!

The story ends happily. Tobias finds a wife, Sarah, 'sensible, brave, and very beautiful' (Tobit 6: 12), and he does not suffer the fate of her seven previous husbands, all of whom died on their wedding night. The heart and liver of the fish are burned, causing a smoke that sends the demon that killed Sarah's seven husbands 'into Upper Egypt' (Tobit 8: 3). Raquel, Sarah's father, gives Tobias half his goods and, to crown all, the gall of the fish rubbed on Tobit's eyes gives him back his sight.

116 *Tobias and the Angel, Tuscan School, National Gallery, London*

Judith

The book of Judith is in the Apocrypha (p. 145). The second part of the story (chapters 8–15) describes a daring episode in which Judith is the heroine, and the first part (chapters 1–7) pretends to give the historic setting of the story. It is impossible, however, to make sense of the historic details in this part of the book, although it is quite likely that the episode in which Judith figures so prominently is based on an incident that actually happened at some time or other. The book in the form in which we now have it was probably written about the middle of the first century B.C.

Judith was a rich young widow, 'a very beautiful and attractive woman' (Judith 8: 7), who was determined to deliver her people from a swaggering tyrant, Holophernes, the chief captain of the Assyrian army. She 'took off her widow's weeds . . . and dressed in her gayest clothes . . . and made herself very attractive, so as to catch the eye of any man who might see her' (Judith 10: 3f.). Then she and her maid approached the Assyrian camp and persuaded the guards to allow them to visit Holophernes in his tent, on the pretext that Judith would 'show him a route by which he can gain command of the entire hill-country without losing a single man' (Judith 10: 13). At the first sight of Judith, Holophernes was 'amazed at the beauty of her face' (Judith 10: 23), and on the fourth day of her stay in the Assyrian camp he made a great feast to which he invited Judith, hoping for an opportunity to seduce her. Holophernes 'drank a great deal of wine, more, indeed, than he had ever drunk on any single day since he was born' (Judith 12: 20). At last Holophernes lay 'sprawled on his bed, dead drunk', and Judith saw her opportunity. She 'took down his sword . . . , grasped his hair . . . , struck at his neck twice with all her might, and cut off his head' (Judith 13: 2, 6–8).

This painting (**117**) by Cristofano Allori (1577–1621) in the Pitti Palace, Florence, shows Judith holding the severed head of Holophernes in her left hand, the sword still in her right hand, and her maid standing by admiringly. Part of the bed upon which Holophernes had been lying is seen in the bottom right hand corner of the picture.

Judith took the head of Holophernes back to her own people, and it was set up for public display. Inspired by Judith's courage, the Jews took fresh heart and put the Assyrians to flight, inflicting on them a great slaughter. Judith was acclaimed a national heroine and the final chapter of the book contains a noble song of praise and thanksgiving sung by Judith, 'in which all the people joined lustily' (Judith 16: 1).

117 *Judith and Holophernes, Cristofano Allori, Pitti Palace, Florence*

TENTS

The Israelites of the early Old Testament period were shepherds by trade, and therefore nomads of necessity. They needed dwellings that were quickly put up, equally quickly taken down, and easily carried from place to place. The tent is almost the only type of dwelling that meets these requirements, and so the Israelites of this period were tent-dwellers.

After the exodus and the conquest of Canaan many of the Israelites gave up the hard nomadic life of the shepherd and took up the more settled life of the farmer, learning from the Canaanites whom they found occupying the land when they returned from Egypt. It was then no longer necessary for them to live in tents, and many of them built simple stone houses on the land they farmed. Nevertheless, the poorer people continued to live in tents, perhaps on the fringe of the towns that sprang up, and the mention of tents in almost every part of the Bible suggests that tent-dwelling continued during the whole of the biblical period. A sect of the Hebrews, the Rechabites, chose for religious reasons to live in tents rather than in houses, but this was exceptional.

No tent of the Old Testament period has survived, needless to say, but a verse in Isaiah helps us to visualize the kind of tent the Hebrews lived in. It says, 'Enlarge the limits of your home, spread wide the curtains of your tent; let out its ropes to

118 *Bedouin tents in the Negeb*

119 *A Bedouin tent near Beersheba*

the full and drive the pegs home' (Isa. 54: 2). Tents used by the Bedouin in the Negeb today (**118**) are probably little different from the tents of Old Testament times. The near view (**119**) shows the details mentioned by Isaiah.

Tents made from branches of trees had, and still have today, a special religious significance for Jews (p. 171), and the Tabernacle (p. 151) was a tent of even greater religious importance.

THE CAMEL

The camel (**120**) merits the description commonly assigned to it: 'the ship of the desert'. Its padded feet do not sink deeply into the sand, it has reserves of water in the walls of its stomach upon which it can draw when crossing a desert, its hump is a storehouse of food, and it has great powers of endurance.

Mention of camels in the early part of the Bible is probably mistaken. This bad-tempered animal was not fully domesticated until after the patriarchal period. The donkey was the usual beast of burden in early Old Testament times (**121**).

120 *Camel transport*

DRESS

Beni Hasan (map **3**) is on the Nile about 106 kilometres (66 miles) south of Cairo. It is famous for the many rock tombs cut in the limestone cliffs which form the eastern bank of the Nile along this stretch of the river. A wall-painting in one of the tombs is illustrated here (**121**). It is dated about 1895 B.C. In the tomb the brightly coloured frieze is in one continuous band, but for economy of space it is shown here in two sections. The inscription along the top describes the scene: thirty-seven Semites bringing eye-paint to Beni Hasan. Semites are the supposed descendants of Shem, and therefore include the Hebrews.

Two Egyptians wearing only white loin cloths lead the procession. Two gazelles follow. Next there are four Semite warriors; two of them wearing long white tunics, the other two wearing embroidered tunics of blue and red. They are armed with bows, spears and throw-sticks shaped like a boomerang. One of them has a skin bottle strapped on his back. A boy wearing red shorts and carrying a spear is walking in front of four women wearing coloured and patterned skirts coming well below the knee. Two men wearing red and white striped kilts bring up the rear. One of them is carrying an eight-stringed lyre which he is playing. The women have black hair bound and hanging down the back, and the men have black hair and pointed beards. The donkeys in the procession have patterned blankets on their backs, and they are carrying objects that are difficult to identify; perhaps goat-skin bellows.

It can be assumed that this finely executed painting represents the general appearance and the formal dress of Hebrew men and women at about the time of the patriarchs and probably for many years after this time.

122 *Ivory comb from Megiddo*

This double ivory comb (**122**), one of several found at Megiddo and dated between 1350 and 1150 B.C., will serve to remind us that both men and women, in Bible times as now, adorned themselves with more than the mere necessities of bodily covering. This beautiful object depicts, on a panel between the two rows of teeth, a lion crouching among trees. The comb would be worn as a decoration on formal occasions. It is on display in the Oriental Institute, the University of Chicago.

WELLS AND WATER

Wells like the one illustrated here (**123**) were sunk in the desert areas of Palestine from earliest times, especially along the caravan routes. Sometimes these wells were the scene of squabbles between rival groups, as when the seven daughters of the priest of Midian came to a well and 'some shepherds came and drove them away' (Exod. 2: 16f.).

Nearness to a spring of water often decided the position of a city, and only after the invention of the cistern for storing water did cities become more or less

123 *A well in the desert*

independent of spring water. The spring used by a city was usually at the foot of the tell (p. 17) and therefore outside the city wall. In time of siege it would be inaccessible to the city dwellers, who in more normal times reached it by a path down the sloping side of the tell. Excavation has shown that difficult engineering feats were sometimes undertaken to bring water into a city.

The spring at Jerusalem was called Gihon and it lies at the foot of the eastern slope of the ancient city of Ophel (map **56**). Charles Warren, an English architect, discovered a vertical shaft half way up the slope of the city mound, probably sunk in about 2000 B.C. It seems to have been a first attempt which had to be abandoned, for it does not reach the water below. A second attempt using a stairway cut in the rock leading to a vertical shaft was successful.

Threatened by an Assyrian attack (p. 87) at the end of the eighth century B.C., Hezekiah hastily strengthened the city defences of Jerusalem and tried to ensure a water supply in case of siege. To do this he 'blocked the upper outflow of the waters of Gihon and directed them downwards and westwards to the city of David' (2 Chron. 32: 30). This probably means that Hezekiah's engineers drove a tunnel from the spring into the city mound on its east side, through the hill, and out again at its west side into the 'Pool of Shelah' (Neh. 3 : 15), later known as the pool of Siloam. The tunnel runs in an S-shaped bend and it is still possible to wade through it from end to end (**124**), a distance of about 530 metres (1739 feet). The pool of Siloam, like Gihon, was outside the city wall. In time of siege Gihon was covered to prevent water flowing from it to the east, and it was also thus hidden from the enemy. Siloam was in the narrow valley that then ran up the west side of Ophel and could easily be defended.

124 *Hezekiah's tunnel*

125 *Inscription from Hezekiah's tunnel*

Native boys playing near the pool of Siloam in 1880 spotted for the first time some writing cut into the side of the tunnel about 6 metres (20 feet) from the entrance. It turned out to be a six-line inscription in Hebrew describing the work of the tunnellers (**125**). In 1890 this wall plaque was cut out of the rock and taken away by vandals (and broken in the process), but it was recovered and it is now in the Museum of the Ancient Orient, Istanbul. The writing is some of the earliest of its kind in our possession. It dates from about 700 B.C., and it tells how the workmen drove the tunnel from opposite ends 'each towards his fellow'. Both parties of workmen had to change direction slightly, and then 'the stone-cutters struck through . . . axe against axe'. The construction of the Siloam tunnel is generally considered to be one of the greatest feats of engineering in ancient times. It was still remembered in the second century B.C., for these words are found in the book of Ecclesiasticus: 'Hezekiah fortified his city, bringing water within its walls; he drilled through the rock with tools of iron and made cisterns for the water' (Ecclus. 48: 17).

THRESHING

Threshing is the process of separating grain from chaff. Beating with a stick on a windy day was sufficient for small quantities of grain in ancient times, but larger quantities required a hard floor, either a flat rock or an artificially prepared surface, on which oxen could walk round and round trampling the grain. For still more efficient threshing the oxen dragged a 'threshing instrument' (so called in earlier English versions of the Bible) over the grain. The New English Bible uses

126 *A threshing floor*

more descriptive terms: 'threshing-sledges' (2 Sam. 24: 22), 'a sharp threshing-sledge . . . studded with teeth' (Isa. 41: 15), 'threshing-sledges spiked with iron' (Amos 1: 3).

A modern threshing floor is illustrated here (**126**). The sledge is horse-drawn and consists of a heavy curved base to the bottom of which are fixed metal spikes. The two boys are evidently enjoying their ride on the roundabout and are at the same time giving extra weight to the sledge to beat out the grain. The horse is not muzzled and it is therefore free to eat some of the grain on the floor. This is in accordance with an ancient law, which says, 'You shall not muzzle an ox while it is treading out the corn' (Deut. 25: 4).

LOCUSTS

The book of Leviticus distinguishes between 'living creatures that may be eaten and living creatures that may not be eaten' (Lev. 11: 47). Among the insects, only those 'that go on four legs' and have their 'legs jointed above their feet for leaping on the ground' (Lev. 11: 20) may be eaten without transgressing the food laws of ancient Israel. Various kinds of locusts figure prominently among these edible insects: 'every kind of great locust, every kind of long-headed locust, every kind of green locust, and every kind of desert locust' (Lev. 11: 22). This photograph (**127**) shows plainly that the locust has six legs, not four, but the very long pair

127 *A locust*

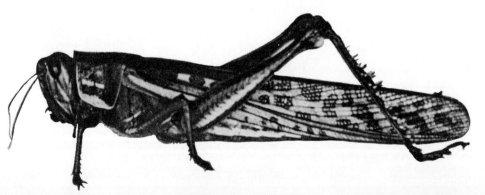

128 *A swarm of locusts*

(they are as long as its body) are used only for jumping and not for walking; so the locust really does 'go on four legs'.

To prepare locusts for eating they are lightly roasted, dried in the sun, and salted. Only the fleshy part is eaten. When John the Baptist was in the wilderness 'he fed on locusts' (Mark 1: 6), and some people living in the Near East today regard them as a delicacy.

The locust has very sharp cutting teeth, and a swarm of locusts (**128**) can quickly reduce a crop to nothing but bare stalks. Immediately before the exodus of the Israelites from Egypt a swarm of this kind, blown by 'a wind roaring in from the east', invaded the countryside so that the locusts 'covered the surface of the whole land till it was black with them', and soon 'there was no green left on tree or plant throughout all Egypt' (Exod. 10: 12–16). Another disastrous plague of locusts occurred at the time of the prophet Joel, and in the first part of his prophecy he describes the havoc it caused. He says that the invading locusts had 'a lion's teeth', and 'the fangs of a lioness', and that they ruined the vines, left fig-trees 'broken and leafless . . . , plucked them bare . . . , left the branches white' (Joel 1: 6f.). He says of a second invasion that it was 'like a countless host in battle array', so destructive that 'nothing survives their march'. Joel takes this terrible plague as the signal that 'the day of the LORD has come' (Joel 2: 1–11).

DYEING

Coloured fabrics are mentioned in several places in the Old Testament, and the manufacture of dyes must have been an important industry in Bible times. These stone troughs (**129**) were found at Byblos in Phoenicia (map **3**), one of the centres of the dyeing trade. They are dated between 3000 and 1600 B.C. Purple dye, the most highly prized, was made from a shell fish, *murex trunculus*, found plentifully on the Phoenician coast. The troughs may have been used for grinding the powdered dye to a fine texture, or for mixing the colouring matter.

LAMPS

In ancient times buildings were illuminated by lamplight, and lamps are among the objects most frequently unearthed by excavators. The shape of a lamp is a valuable clue to the date of the stratum in which it is found (pp. 17f.). This saucer-type lamp (**130**), dated about the fourteenth century B.C., was found at Hazor (map **1**). It is made of earthenware, and has a lip in which the wick rested with its lower end dipping in the oil. When saucer-type lamps are found they frequently show several carbon deposits round the rim, and this suggests that sometimes more than one wick was used to give a brighter light. Other excavated lamps have several lips pinched out round the rim to hold several wicks. Seven seems to have been a favourite number, and the 'seven pipes each for the lamps' referred to in Zech. 4: 2 (footnote) may be an allusion to seven-wick lamps, like those illustrated in Howland's model of Solomon's temple (**179**). The 'lamp-stands of red gold, five

130 *A saucer-type lamp*

on the right side and five on the left side' (1 Kings 7: 49) are also seen in this model.

Olive oil was the usual illuminant; the commonest kind for household lamps, and 'pure oil of pounded olives', which the Israelites were commanded to supply, for the 'Tent of the Presence' (Exod. 27: 20f.). Wick was probably made of twisted flax. The 'capable wife . . . never puts out her lamp at night' (Prov. 31: 10, 18), because of the difficulty of relighting a lamp before the invention of matches.

Lamps of the Greek period and later usually had the oil reservoir covered, with two holes in the cover: one for filling the lamp with oil and the other to hold the wick.

SEAFARING

The Hebrews were not a maritime people, although the sea forms the entire western boundary of Palestine. The ships in Solomon's fleet (p. 62) were probably manned by Phoenician sailors. The cedar and pine wood needed for the building of Solomon's temple was made into rafts and floated by seamen of Tyre from the coast of Lebanon (map 3) 'to the roadstead at Joppa' (2 Chron. 2: 16), and the wood for the second temple was brought by 'the Sidonians and the Tyrians' in the same way (Ezra 3: 7).

This shaped stone (131) was used as an anchor by Phoenician seamen in the eighteenth century B.C. The groove made in the stone by the friction of the anchor rope can be seen above the hole through which the rope passed.

131 *A Phoenician anchor at Byblos*

MUSIC

Music, both vocal and instrumental, was used from primitive times in religious ceremonial, in military exercises, and as a recreational activity. In the earliest reference to music in the Bible, Jubal is said to be 'the ancestor of those who play the harp and pipe' (Gen. 4: 21).

Archaeologists have discovered a number of pictorial representations of ancient musical instruments, and in a few places have unearthed the remains of actual instruments. The wall-painting in the tomb at Beni Hasan (**121**) shows an eight-stringed lyre being played by a musician using a plectrum, which is not visible in the photograph. The painting is dated about 1895 B.C., but the lyre was in use earlier than this, for no fewer than four of these instruments were found in the great death-pit in the royal cemetery at Ur, dated about 2500 B.C. The finest of them is decorated with red, white and blue mosaic work, gold and silver bands, and a splendid bull's head of gold on the sounding box. It is on display in the Babylonian Room of the British Museum.

An instrument identical with the golden lyre of Ur may be seen in this illustration of the standard of Ur (**132**). This object was found by C. L. Woolley in the royal cemetery lying near the shoulder of a man, who may have carried it as a standard (hence the name commonly given to it) into battle or on ceremonial occasions. It has brightly coloured mosaic pictures on both sides in rows almost like a strip cartoon. Its removal from the ground without damage was a delicate operation, and its restoration was a skilful piece of craftsmanship. It is now in the Babylonian Room of the British Museum. The side shown here probably depicts

132 *The standard of Ur*

133 *The blind harpist*

a victory celebration, and the other side represents various aspects of warfare. At the banquet the king, distinguished by his greater height than the other members of the party, is seen on the left of the top row. He wears a wide, highly decorated skirt and faces six evidently eminent guests. The king and his guests are seated on chairs and they hold cups in their right hands. To the right of this row are a musician playing a lyre and a woman singer with long black hair. The bull's head on the sounding box of the lyre can be plainly seen, and the position of the woman's hands suggests that the song she is singing is a sentimental one. The lower rows of pictures show either the spoils of war or supplies of food for the banquet being brought in.

The harp is usually larger than the lyre and often has a greater number of strings. This delicate and beautiful relief (**133**) originally formed part of a representation of a solemn funeral ceremony carved on the limestone walls of a mortuary chapel at Karnak. It is dated about 1400 B.C. and it may now be seen in the Museum of Antiquities at Leiden, Holland. The harp has a large sounding box, and eight strings which are being plucked by both hands of the player. The curved frame has tuning pegs at the top, one for each string. The harpist is blind.

'Trumpets made from rams' horns' (Josh. 6: 4) were blown when Joshua's army attacked Jericho (**50**), and a ram's horn is still in use today in every Jewish synagogue (pp. 163ff.). It gives out a shrill note that is not particularly pleasing to the ear. Lists of musical instruments in the Bible, for example, 'lute, harp, fife, and drum' (1 Sam. 10: 5), 'horns and trumpets, clashing cymbals . . . , lutes and harps' (1 Chron. 15: 28), 'horn, pipe, zither, triangle, dulcimer' (Dan. 3: 5), make it clear that a full range of strings, wind, and percussion instruments was in use in the temple services and on other ceremonial occasions.

COINS

Coinage was not introduced into Palestine until the Persian period. Before that time, pieces of silver (gold rarely) of known weight were used as means of trade and exchange. Amos noticed that the dishonest traders of Bethel used 'overweight in the silver' with which they weighed out the customers' bits of metal (Amos 8: 5). The custom of stamping the weight on a piece of metal used as money may be the origin of the markings found on coins from earliest times until now.

Coins of the Old Testament period are illustrated here (**134** to **154**) in their actual size. All the coins, except **140**, are in the Fitzwilliam Museum, Cambridge, and the photographs have been taken direct from the coins. The notes on them have been generously supplied by the Reverend H. St J. Hart, Queens' College, Cambridge. They are illustrated here by kind permission of the Syndics of the Fitzwilliam Museum. Number **140** is photographed from an electrotype copy in the British Museum.

134. A silver siglos, or half Babylonian stater, minted at Sardis. On one side, heads of a lion and a bull; on the other side, a stamped design. Coins like this one were issued by Croesus of Lydia (561–546 B.C.) and in the early years of the Persian Empire.

135. A silver daric of Darius III (338–331 B.C.). On one side, the king with bow, quiver, and spear; on the other side, a stamped design. Coins like this one were issued from the time of Darius I (522–486 B.C.) for use in the western parts of the Persian Empire.

136. A silver stater minted at Tarsus in Cilicia, then held by the Persians under the satrap, Mazdai (about 361–333 B.C.). On one side, Baal enthroned, with a long sceptre, a bunch of grapes and an ear of corn; on the other side, a lion attacking a bull, above a representation of the battlements of Tarsus. Legend in Semitic: 'The Baal of Tarsus'.

137. A silver stater of Byblos in Phoenicia; fourth century B.C. On one side, a galley with warriors and a sea monster; on the other side, a lion attacking a bull. Legend in Phoenician: 'Azba'al king of Byblos'.

138. A silver double shekel of Sidon in Phoenicia; about 384–370 B.C. On one side, a war galley; on the other side, the king in a chariot with driver and an attendant.

139. A silver stater of Tyre; about 400–332 B.C. On one side, Melkart, the Phoenician Baal, riding on a sea monster, with a dolphin under the water; on the other side, a bird, a crook and a flail.

140. A silver coin of the fourth century B.C. On one side, a bearded warrior with helmet; on the other side, a deity on a winged chariot holding a bird. Legend in Aramaic: YHD (that is, Jehud, the official Aramaic name of the district).

141. A silver tetradrachm minted at Tarsus; about 327–324 B.C. On one side, the head of Herakles; on the other side, Zeus enthroned, with eagle and sceptre. Legend in Greek: 'Of Alexander'.

142. A silver tetradrachm minted at Acco, similar to **141**.

143. A silver stater minted at Sidon. On one side, the head of Athena, goddess of wisdom; on the other side, a winged Victory. Legend: 'Of Alexander'.

144. A silver tetradrachm minted at Alexandria, similar to **141**.

145

146

147

148

149

150

151

152

153

154

145. A silver tetradrachm minted at Alexandria, similar to **144**.

146. A silver tetradrachm minted at Alexandria, similar to **145** but with a thunderbolt beneath the bird.

147. A silver tetradrachm minted at Babylon, similar to **146**. Legend in Greek: 'Of king Philip' (that is, Philip III).

148. A silver tetradrachm. On one side, a portrait of Alexander the Great; on the other side, Athena enthroned, holding Victory. Legend in Greek: 'Of king Lysimachus' (that is, Lysimachus of Thrace).

149. A silver tetradrachm of Egypt in the time of Ptolemy I (323–304 B.C.). On one side, the head of Alexander-Herakles; on the other side, Zeus enthroned, with eagle and sceptre. Legend in Greek: 'Of Alexander'.

150. A silver tetradrachm, perhaps minted at Ephesus. On one side, the head of Ptolemy I as king; on the other side, an eagle on a thunderbolt. Legend in Greek: 'Of Ptolemy Soter' (that is, Ptolemy III).

151. A silver tetradrachm minted at Sidon. Note the ΣΙ, that is, 'Sidon', between the eagle's legs. On one side, the head of the young king, Ptolemy V (204–181 B.C.); on the other side, an eagle on a thunderbolt. Legend in Greek: 'Of king Ptolemy'.

152. A silver tetradrachm minted at Antioch on the Orontes. On one side, a portrait of Antiochus III the Great; on the other side, Apollo, with bow and arrow, seated on the omphalos, a conical stone supposed to be the central point of the earth. Legend in Greek: 'Of king Antiochus'.

153. A silver tetradrachm minted at Antioch. On one side, the head of Antiochus IV Epiphanes; on the other side, Apollo seated on the omphalos (see **152**). Legend in Greek: 'Of king Antiochus'.

154. A silver tetradrachm minted at Antioch. On one side, the head of Zeus; on the other side, Zeus enthroned, holding Victory. Legend in Greek: 'Of king Antiochus, god-manifest, bearing Victory'.

Readers wishing to learn more about the coins of the Old Testament period should consult *The Use of Coin Types and Legends in Biblical Studies*, which is in preparation, by H. St J. Hart.

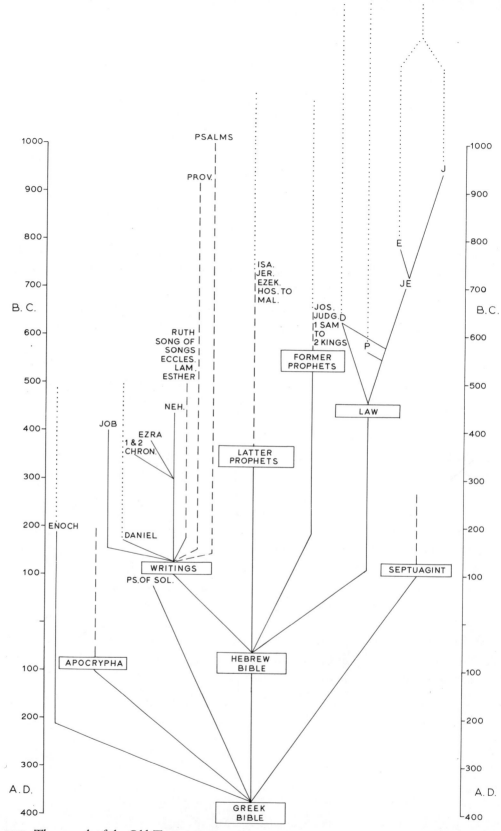

155 *The growth of the Old Testament*

THE GROWTH OF THE OLD TESTAMENT

This diagram (**155**) is an attempt to show how the Old Testament came into being. A dotted line (. . . . .) represents the period during which the material was passed on by word of mouth from one generation to the next; a broken line (- - - - -) represents the period during which this oral material was put into writing; and a full line (————) represents the period during which this written material was passed on from one generation to the next. The oral period goes back much further than can be shown on the diagram, probably to a time not much later than the settlement of the Hebrews in Canaan after the exodus (pp. 52ff.).

Some of the suggested dates are open to question, partly because complete agreement about them has not yet been reached by Old Testament scholars. The date given for the completed Hebrew Bible (about A.D. 100) is that of a conference held at Jamnia (map **1**) to decide officially which books to include and which to exclude. It is probable, however, that unofficial agreement had been reached long before this date. The date suggested for the Greek Bible (fourth century A.D.) is that of the earliest copies of it we now possess (pp. 144f.), but almost certainly there were earlier Greek Bibles which have not survived.

In the Hebrew Bible the individual books are arranged in three groups: the Law, the Prophets, and the Writings. The same books are also found in the English Bible, but in a different order. For our purpose it is convenient to retain the grouping of the Hebrew Bible, and this has been done in the diagram.

The Law (or Torah, the Hebrew word for 'teaching') consists of the first five books in the Old Testament (Genesis, Exodus, Leviticus, Numbers and Deuteronomy), and it is therefore sometimes called the Pentateuch (*pente* is Greek for 'five'). Detailed study of the Pentateuch suggests that it grew in compilation in some such way as a cathedral grows in building. The parts of an old cathedral have usually been built at different times, and it is not uncommon to see, for example, a Norman west door, a Gothic nave, a Renaissance choir, and so on, in the same building. Similarly, the parts of the Law seem to have been written at different times. The earliest material (J) uses Yahweh (Jahveh in Latin, hence the symbol J) for the name of God; the next earliest (E) uses Elohim for the name of God; the next (D) corresponds roughly to the book of Deuteronomy as we know it today; whilst the latest material (P) is specially concerned with the part played by the priests in the ceremonial of worship. J and E material is scattered in various parts of Genesis, Exodus and Numbers; D material is mainly found in Deuteronomy, but traces of it are also found in Exodus and Numbers, and its influence is felt in the Former Prophets; P material is found mainly in Leviticus, but there are also traces of it in the other four books of the Law.

The books of the Former Prophets (Joshua, Judges, and the books of Samuel and Kings) look at first sight like Hebrew history books, but a closer look shows that in addition to a record of events, they give an interpretation of the events they describe. This interpretation was added long after the events themselves, and it was an application of the teaching of the prophets of a later period. The Hebrews thought it quite legitimate to call these books of combined history and interpretation, the Former Prophets; and the books containing the teaching on which the interpretation was based, the Latter Prophets.

The diagram helps to make clear a number of matters in connection with the Writings. (i) The memoirs of Nehemiah and the memoirs of Ezra were eventually combined with 1 and 2 Chronicles to form a complete work. (ii) Daniel is one of the latest books in the Old Testament, but the writer used stories from a much earlier period. (iii) The five rolls (Ruth, Esther, Ecclesiastes, Song of Songs, and Lamentations) are grouped together in spite of their obvious differences. The explanation is that they are the books associated with the Jewish festivals (p. 169). Enoch and the Psalms of Solomon were included in the Greek Bible, but they never found a place in either the Hebrew Bible or the Apocrypha.

Interesting and important cross-references might have been included in this diagram, but this would have made it unduly complicated. Similarly, the books grouped together in the diagram (for example, the Prophets) might have been separated according to their dates, but this also would have made it too detailed and unclear. If the reader requires additional information, he must consult the standard textbooks on the subject.

HEBREW MANUSCRIPTS

A copy of the Law for use in a synagogue must be in Hebrew and written by hand on the skin of an animal considered by orthodox Jews to be clean; that is, 'any animal which has a parted foot or a cloven hoof and also chews the cud' (Lev. 11: 3). Hebrew is read from right to left and in the case of the synagogue scrolls of the Law it is written without vowels or spaces between the words. One of the names for God, for example, was written YHWH. The Law forbids the utterance of this name: 'Whoever utters the Name of the LORD shall be put to death' (Lev. 24: 16). The word was therefore never pronounced, and when it occurred the reader substituted another word, Adonai, meaning 'Lord'. When the vowels were eventually attached to YHWH, they were the vowels of Adonai, and the name, when Anglicized, became Jehovah. It is probable that the original

156 *Scribe copying the Law*

form of YHWH with the vowels added was YaHWeH, now usually written Yahweh.

The work of copying the Hebrew Bible (**156**) calls for considerable skill and very great accuracy, for not even the most minute error can be tolerated. There are special precautions to prevent mistakes creeping in, and elaborate regulations for the scribe to observe. For example, he is required to take a bath before beginning to write, and he must not begin to write the name of God with a pen freshly dipped in the ink, lest taking his eyes from the page should cause him to lose the place and copy the wrong word or the correct word in the wrong place.

In the spring of 1947 some scrolls wrapped in damp-proof linen coverings were accidentally discovered in a cave at Qumran near the Dead Sea (map **I**). Many more caves were later found in the same area and more scrolls and fragments of parchment were discovered in them. These important finds are now known collectively as the Dead Sea scrolls or the Qumran scrolls, and some of them are dated as early as the second century B.C. This scroll (**157**) is the most complete and the most important of them. It is a complete copy of the book of Isaiah written on vellum made from the skins of clean animals. Seventeen skins have been stitched together using as thread the gut of a clean animal. The stitching can be seen to the left of the exposed text and on the right-hand side roll. The scroll is open at Isaiah 40. A correction can be seen on the seventh line from the top of the left-hand column. Both the rolls are soiled where they have been handled by many readers in the past.

157 *Scroll of Isaiah from Qumran*

There are many minor differences between the text of this manuscript of Isaiah and the manuscripts we possessed before its discovery. The scroll is about a thousand years earlier, and it may therefore be assumed to be free from the errors that would have been introduced by repeated copying during that period. English versions of the Bible made after about 1950 (the Revised Standard Version, the Jerusalem Bible, and the New English Bible) have used the scroll to produce a more accurate and a more meaningful text in several places in the book of Isaiah. The footnotes indicate that more than fifty readings from the scroll have been introduced in the text of the book of Isaiah in the New English Bible.

Fragments of every book in the Old Testament except Esther have been found in the caves at Qumran. The scrolls and fragments may be the remains of the library of the Essenes, a pious community of people who lived in the monastery near the caves. If so, they may have excluded Esther from their collection of books because it does not contain the name of God. The Qumran scrolls are now magnificently housed in the Shrine of the Book at the Hebrew University of Jerusalem.

This Hebrew manuscript (**158**) is one of the earliest we possessed before the discovery of the Qumran scrolls. It was written in the early part of the tenth century A.D. and it is now in the British Museum. The text shown here is Lev. 5:18–6:5, and it represents a page of a book, not part of a scroll. Vowel marks can

158 *Hebrew manuscript of the tenth century*

be seen under some of the letters, and there is a full commentary on the text at the top and the bottom of the page, and an abbreviated commentary in the margins to the left of the columns. Occasionally a commentator introduced a variation into his work by writing his notes on the text in the form of a line-drawing made up of Hebrew letters. This manuscript (**159**) in the British Museum is a pleasant example of this practice.

159 *Hebrew manuscript with commentary*

160 *Nablus at the foot of Mount Gerizim*

THE SAMARITAN PENTATEUCH

The city of Nablus was built by Vespasian in A.D. 72 on a site near Shechem (map 1), where the Samaritans had lived since their expulsion from Samaria by Alexander the Great in about 331 B.C. This photograph (**160**) shows the position of Nablus at the foot of Mount Gerizim. About a hundred Samaritans still live at Nablus, and they have in their synagogue a valuable copy of the Pentateuch. It is seen here (**161**) in charge of two Samaritan priests. The biblical text is in small print in the middle of the scroll, and the large print on the covers of the rolls is not part of it. The Samaritans claim that this copy of the Pentateuch was written by Abisha, the great-grandson of Moses, but this is certainly not true. Recent examination of the manuscript shows, however, that it may be older than used to be thought. Similarities between the Exodus of the Samaritan Pentateuch and a portion of Exodus found among the Qumran scrolls reinforces that opinion. The Samaritan Pentateuch at Nablus may have been written before the Christian era; but it must be admitted that the origin and the early history of this manuscript is obscure. The original from which the copies in our possession have been made was probably written in the time of Nehemiah, say about 400 B.C. It is estimated that there are about 6000 differences, most of them minor, between the Samaritan and the Hebrew Pentateuchs.

161 *The Samaritan Pentateuch at Nablus*

THE SEPTUAGINT

The Hebrews have always been wanderers, and in late Old Testament times there were Jews in many parts of the known world. They had left Palestine under economic stress, in search of trade, or in retreat under persecution. The Elephantine papyri (pp. 99ff.) show that there was a colony of Jews in Egypt in the sixth century B.C. After the foundation of Alexandria (map **3**) many Jews settled in that city, where Greek was the language commonly spoken. The time came when these Alexandrian Jews could read and speak Greek more easily than Hebrew, and it became necessary for them to have their scriptures in Greek. Fanciful stories tell of a letter taken from Alexandria to Jerusalem begging the high priest to send a copy of the Hebrew Bible and men to translate it, so that a Greek version of it could be placed in the great library at Alexandria. The story goes on to say that six translators from each of the twelve tribes went to Alexandria, taking with them a copy of the Law written in letters of gold. In some versions of the story each of the 72 men worked independently in separate cells, and in exactly 72 days produced 72 identical translations! The name 'Septuagint' and the symbol often used to represent it (LXX) echo the numerical part of this fantastic story (*septuaginta* is Latin for 'seventy'). The truth probably is that a Greek version of the Law was first produced, perhaps in the third century B.C., and that the other books were added later by different translators at different times (diagram **155**). The final form of the Greek Bible contains not only the books of our Old Testament, but also the books of the Apocrypha; that is, the books that were excluded from the Hebrew Bible when its contents were decided at the conference at Jamnia (p. 137). Almost certainly the Septuagint was the Bible used by Paul and the early Church.

The earliest copies we possess of the Septuagint are large volumes that were compiled in the fourth and fifth centuries A.D. This one (**162**) is the famous Codex Sinaiticus, one of the most valuable exhibits in the British Museum. It was written on fine quality vellum in the middle of the fourth century A.D., and was found by Tischendorf in 1844 in the monastery of St Catherine at Mount Sinai (hence the name given to it). Its pages are 37 centimetres (nearly 15 inches) by 34 centimetres (about 13 inches), and there are four columns to a page, except in the poetry sections of the Old Testament, where there are two columns to a page. In this illustration (**162**) the volume is open at Ps. 19: 8 – 23: 5 (corresponding to Ps. 20: 7 – 24: 5 in the English book of Psalms).

THE MAZARIN BIBLE

Until the middle of the fifteenth century A.D. the copying of manuscripts was done by hand, with the inevitable introduction of errors. Then the art of printing was discovered by Gutenberg and in 1454 there appeared the first sheet of print. It was made on the printing press at Mainz in Germany, and it was here also that in 1456 the Bible in Latin was produced; the first complete printed book. This was an important event, for it ensured that no longer need copying errors be multiplied and no longer need Bibles be restricted in circulation by the laborious, expensive and time-consuming operation of hand copying.

The Septuagint was translated into Latin, the language used by educated scholars, and this added still another to the several existing Latin versions of the text, some of them far from perfect. In about A.D. 382 Pope Damasus invited Jerome, the best biblical scholar of his day, to end the confusion by producing a standard Latin version of the Bible to replace the many imperfect versions that were in circulation. His version is known as the Vulgate, because it was a 'vulgar' translation intended for 'the man in the street' (Latin, *vulgus*: the common people).

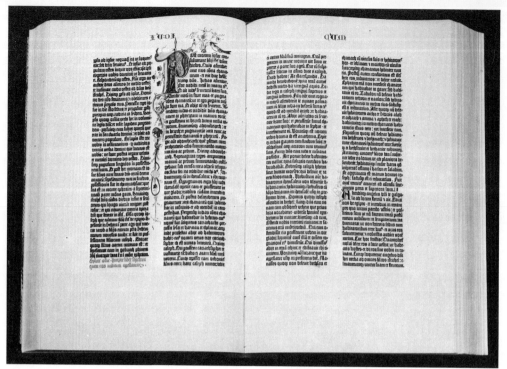

It was Jerome's Latin Vulgate that became the first complete printed book. It is known as the Mazarin Bible because the copy of it that first received the attention of scholars was in the library of Cardinal Mazarin in Paris. This facsimile of it (**163**) is in the Library of the British and Foreign Bible Society, London. The book of Judges begins with the illuminated letter at the head of the second column on the left hand page. An original copy of the Mazarin Bible, once owned by George III, may be seen in the King's Library at the British Museum.

THE COVERDALE BIBLE

Hand-written translations into English of parts of the Bible were made from the eighth century A.D. onwards, and a complete version of the Bible in English, that made by Wycliffe and his colleagues, appeared in 1388. William Tyndale produced the first printed New Testament in English at Worms in Germany, and it reached England a year later. Tyndale also began a translation of the Old Testament, but he never completed it. The work done by Tyndale on the Old Testament was used by Miles Coverdale, who gave us the first complete printed Bible in English in 1535.

This page of Coverdale's Bible (**164**) shows the beginning of the Old Testament, with illustrations of the six days of Creation as they are described in Genesis 1 and 2. God is represented in the form of a man (pp. 24f.) and the subjects are treated naively. Coverdale included in his Bible a translation of the Apocrypha (p. 145).

In the Greek Bible the books of the Apocrypha are mixed among the rest of the Old Testament, but Coverdale brought them together and printed them at the end of his Old Testament. The next illustration (**165**) shows a page from his version of the Apocrypha. It contains the opening verses of Ecclesiasticus, called here 'The Boke of Wyszdome'. Both the illustrations of Coverdale's Bible are from a copy in the Library of the British and Foreign Bible Society, London.

The boke of Wyszdome.

What this boke conteyneth.

Chap. I. An exortaciō for iudges and rulers to loue wyszdome. The sprete of wyszdome hareth falsede, diſſimulacion and ypocriſie, rebuketh vnrighteouſneſſe and abhorreth wicked doers.

Chap. II. The ymaginaciōs and thoughtes of the vngodly, how they geue thē ſelues ouer vnto ſynne, and perſecute all vertue and trueth.

Chap. III. The felicite and health of godly people, though they be put here to trouble and heuyneſſe: Agayne, what ſorow ſhall happen to the vngodly and their children.

Chap. IIII. To lyue chaſt & godly withall, is cōmendable. A diſprayſe of the wicked. The honoure of verteous age. The ſhamefull death of the vngodly.

Chap. V. How the iuſt men ſhal ſtōde againſt the wicked, that haue put them here to trouble & what ſorow ſhall come vpon the vngodly. Agayne, what ioye ſhal happen to the righteous, which haue God himſelf for their defēce.

Chap. VI. An exortacion vnto ſoch as be in rule and auctorite, to receaue wyſdome. A commēdaciō of wyſdome.

Chap. VII. All men haue life intraūce in to the worlde: yet who ſo calleth vpon God for wyſdome, ſhal haue his deſyre. The profit that cōmeth by wyſdome paſſeth all other thinges.

Chap. VIII. Wiſdome ſhulde be receaued in youth. He that marieth himſelf vnto her, ſhall optayne loue of God and men.

Chap. IX. A prayer vnto God for the gift of wyſdome.

Chap. X. What profit and good came by wyſdome in the olde tyme.

Chap. XI. How wiſdome ledeth the righteous, & how the vngodly are punyſhed thorow the mightie hande of God.

Chap. XII. God is mercifull and ſuffreth longe, to the intent that ſynners ſhulde amende.

Chap. XIII. Vayne are they that haue not the knowlege of the lyuynge God, but turne vnto the creatures: vnhappie are they that honoure ymages.

Chap. XIIII. The worſhippinge of ymages. The power of God. Punyſhment of them that make ymages, and of ſoch as worſhipe them. How ymages came vp firſt. The honouringe of ymages is the cauſe, begynnynge, and ende of all myſchefe.

Chap. XV. The faithfull haue reſpecte vnto God and not vnto ymages.

Chap. XVI. God puniſheth the wicked, but defendeth the godly, & that by greate wonders.

Chap. XVII. Of the greate darckneſſe in Egipte, and blyndneſſe of the vngodly.

Chap. XVIII. How God deſtroied the firſtborne of Egipte. Gods people eate the eaſter lambe ioyfully, the Egiptians mourne, God punyſheth the ſynners in the wilderneſſe, Moſes intreateth for the people.

Chap. XIX. Life as the wicked are euer ſynnynge more and more, ſo doth the wrath of God neuer ceaſſe, tyll they be deſtroyed. Of them that were punyſhed in the tyme of Loth.

The firſt Chapter.

SEt youre affeccion vpō wyſdome, ye that be iudges of the earth, haue a good opinion of the LORDE, & ſeke him in the ſynglenneſſe of hert. For he will be founde of them that tempte him not, and appeareth vnto ſoch as put their truſt in him. As for frowarde thoughtes, they ſeparate from God, but vertue (yf it be alowed) refourmeth & vnwyſe. And why? wyſdome ſhall not entre in to a frowarde ſoule, ner dwell in the body that is ſubdued vnto ſynne. For the holy gooſt abhorreth fayned nurtoure, & withdraweth himſelf frō ý thoughtes that are without vnderſtondinge: & where wickednes hath the vpper hāde, he flieth from thence. For the ſprete of wyſdome is louynge, gentle and gracious, and wil haue no pleaſure in him that ſpeaketh euell with his lippes. For God is a witneſſe of his reynes, a true ſearcher out of his hert, and an hearer of his tonge. For the ſprete of ý LORDE fylleth the rounde compaſſe of the worlde, and ý ſame that vpholdeth all thinges, hath knowlege alſo of the voyce.

Therfore he that ſpeaketh vnrighteous thinges, can not be hydd, nether maye he eſcape the iudgmēt of reprofe. And why? inquyſicion ſhal be made for the thoughtes of the vngodly, and the reporte of his wordes ſhal come vnto God, ſo that his wickdnes ſhalbe puniſhed. For the eare of gelouſy heareth all thinges, and the noyſe of the grudginges ſhal not be hydd. Therfore beware of murmuringe, which is nothinge worth, and refrayne youre tonge frō ſlaūder. For there is no worde ſo darck and ſecrete, that it ſhal go for naught: and the mouth that ſpeaketh lyes, ſlayeth the ſoule.

O ſeke not youre owne death in ý erroure of youre life, deſtroye not youre ſelues thorow the workes of youre awne handes. For God hath not made death, nether hath he pleaſure in the deſtruccion of the lyuynge.

S ij

THE GENEVA BIBLE

One effect of the Reformation was to stress the importance of the scriptures, and in 1541 by order of Thomas Cromwell a copy of the Bible was set up in every church in the land. Soon, however, a strong Catholic reaction broke out against the principles of the Reformation. Many Bibles were destroyed and the people were forbidden to read the scriptures either in public or in private. During the reign of Mary this reaction reached a climax. The Bibles were removed from the churches, and many fugitives fled from the Catholic persecution. Among those who settled in Geneva were a group of English scholars, who set to work on a complete revision of the English Bible, and in 1560 their new translation, the Geneva Bible, made its first appearance.

A page from the Geneva Bible of 1560 in the Library of the British and Foreign Bible Society, London, is shown here (**166**). Several interesting features of this revision can be seen in the picture, especially if it is compared with that of Coverdale's Bible (**164**). Comments were added in the margins of the Geneva Bible, some of them strongly reflecting the views of John Calvin and his followers; the chapters were divided into numbered verses for the first time in an English Bible; a few black and white illustrations were included; and the text was printed in small but readable Roman type instead of the large black type of the earlier versions of the Bible, and this made possible the production of a smaller book which was more suitable for personal use at home than any previous English Bible had been.

The Geneva Bible is sometimes called the 'Breeches Bible', because of its unusual translation of Gen. 3:7. This curious verse can be seen near the bottom of the right-hand column in the illustration.

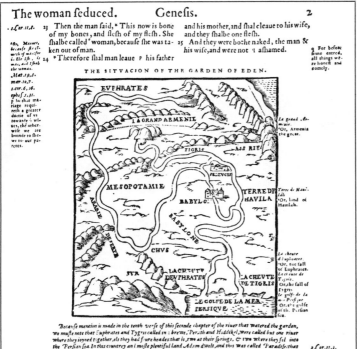

166 *The Geneva Bible*

THE COMPUTER-SET BIBLE

To bring the subject of the growth of the Bible up to date, the computer-set Bible must be mentioned. In 1968 the first Bible of this kind was produced: the Revised Standard Version with black and white illustrations by Horace Knowles, printed for the British and Foreign Bible Society. Some readers may be interested in a few technical details.

The text was first put on punched tape, of which $10\frac{1}{4}$ miles were required for the whole Bible. This was then converted into magnetic tape at the remarkable rate of 500 characters per second. This tape, together with setting instructions for chapter and verse numbers, subtitles, spaces for the illustrations, etc., was then fed into an ICT 1500 computer, which automatically produced printed proof sheets at the rate of 1000 numbered lines per minute. The computer corrected the proofs, produced a final magnetic tape, and set the entire book. Printing and binding were done by the usual means.

The whole Bible and the setting instructions are contained on two rolls of magnetic tape in the metal containers seen in the illustration (**167**). Part of the computer is in the background, and there is a length of punched tape in the foreground.

167 *The computer-set Bible*

THE ARK OF THE TOKENS

The ruins of a synagogue of about A.D. 200 are to be seen at a place on the north-west shore of the Sea of Galilee, which may be the site of biblical Capernaum. Many of the stones of this ruin are richly carved, and this example (**168**) may be a representation of a Roman wagon, but some scholars think it may illustrate the Ark of the Tokens, the 'chest of acacia-wood, two and a half cubits long, one cubit and a half wide, and one cubit and a half high' that was covered 'with pure gold, both inside and out' (Exod. 37: 1f; a cubit is a little less than half a metre, perhaps about 18 inches). The description of the Ark speaks of 'poles in the rings at the sides of the Ark to lift it' (Exod. 37: 5), but this carving may represent the Ark being carried on a cart, perhaps an illustration of the occasion when the Philistines returned the Ark to the Israelites on 'a new wagon' drawn by 'two milch-cows' (I Sam. 6: 7).

The Ark was made to hold 'the Tokens' (Exod. 40: 20), the two tablets of stone on which were written the terms of the convenant with God made by Moses. Before it was put in the temple at Jerusalem, it is said that the Ark was housed in the Tabernacle, the sacred tent consisting of 'ten hangings of finely woven linen, and violet, purple, and scarlet yarn . . . all made by a seamster' (Exod. 36: 8).

168 *Carving at Capernaum*

169 *The hill-shrine at Petra*

HILL-SHRINES AND ALTARS

From earliest times men believed that their gods lived on hill tops, and in Old Testament times some hill tops were still considered to be specially sacred and were used as places of worship. In particular they were thought to be suitable for the offering of sacrifices. In the New English Bible these hill-top sites are called 'hill-shrines', but in most other English versions they are called 'high places'. This photograph (**169**) is of the hill-shrine at Petra, which was probably associated with a Nabataean deity (p. 112). The rock in the foreground served as the altar on which the sacrifices were offered. Note the steps leading to the altar, and the arrangement for draining away the blood of the slaughtered animals. A rock altar of this kind was an important object in Solomon's temple at Jerusalem (**176**).

The Israelites were commanded to destroy the hill-shrines that had been used for pagan worship; and Josiah, for example, in his reforming zeal, 'desecrated the

170 *The hill-shrine at Megiddo*

hill-shrines where they had burnt sacrifices, from Geba to Beersheba, and dismantled the hill-shrines of the demons' (2 Kings 23 : 8). He also 'desecrated the hill-shrines which Solomon the king of Israel had built for Ashtoreth the loathsome goddess of the Sidonians, and for Kemosh the loathsome god of Moab, and for Milcom the abominable god of the Ammonites' (2 Kings 23 : 13).

The altar of the hill-shrine at Megiddo (**170**) stands about two metres (six and a half feet) high and is nearly 10 metres (nearly 33 feet) in diameter. Animals were slaughtered and their bodies were burnt on the raised circular hearth. When it was excavated, animal bones were found at the foot of the steps leading to the altar. This is a Canaanite altar, which was probably in use about 1900 B.C.

Human, as well as animal, sacrifice was occasionally practised in Israel. Ahaz and Manasseh are the two kings who are said to have been guilty of this terrible crime. The former 'burnt sacrifices in the Valley of Ben-hinnom; he even burnt his sons in the fire according to the abominable practice of the nations whom the LORD had dispossessed in favour of the Israelites' (2 Chron. 28 : 3). Manasseh 'made his sons pass through the fire in the Valley of Ben-hinnom' (2 Chron. 33 : 6). This photograph (**171**) shows the Hinnom Valley as it is today (map **56**).

171 *The Hinnom Valley, Jerusalem*

Jeremiah denounced the 'shrine of Topheth in the Valley of Ben-hinnom', where the Israelites burnt 'their sons as whole-offerings to Baal' (Jer. 7: 31, 19: 5); and Josiah desecrated Topheth 'so that no one might make his son or daughter pass through the fire in honour of Molech' (2 Kings 23: 10).

Another kind of altar was perhaps more common in Israel than used to be thought. In several passages in the Law and the Prophets a word that the Revised Version translates 'sun-image' will be found in the New English Bible translated 'incense-altar', and the latter is almost certainly the correct meaning of the word. Evidently incense-altars were fairly common objects in Old Testament times, for small altars with projections at the corners have been excavated at various places in Palestine. An altar of this kind (**172**) was found at Megiddo. It is made of limestone, stands about half a metre (nearly 20 inches) high, and is dated about 1000 B.C. It can be seen in the Palestine Archaeological Museum, Jerusalem. The projections at the corners of an altar are called horns, and they were to be smeared with the blood of the victim when a sacrifice was offered. They also served as refuges to which offenders clung for safety from punishment. It is recorded, for example, that Adonijah 'in fear of Solomon, sprang up and went to the altar and caught hold of its horns' (1 Kings 1: 50).

Incense was burnt in Israelite religious ritual; for example, an incense-altar stood in the sanctuary of the temple before the veil (**179**) and incense was burnt on it each night and morning. Incense-altars used for heathen worship were to be destroyed. King Asa, for example, 'suppressed . . . the incense-altars in all the cities', and this was considered by the writer of Chronicles to be 'good and right in the eyes of the LORD' (2 Chron. 14: 5, 2).

172 *Incense altar from Megiddo*

173 *Bas-relief of Baal*

BAAL

This limestone bas-relief (**173**) is a representation of the Canaanite Baal. It was found at Ras Shamra (ancient Ugarit: map **3**) in 1932 in the sanctuary to the west of the great temple. Its date is variously given by scholars between 1500 B.C. and 1900 B.C., and it is exhibited in the Louvre, Paris.

Baal (ba'al) is not a proper name, but a word meaning lord, or one who possesses rights, and it is frequently used for 'husband'. It is also a general name for 'god', and it is often so used in the Old Testament. Inscribed tablets found at Ras Shamra tell us that El was the chief Canaanite god, and that Asherah was his wife. Their son, a Baal, was the god who controlled the weather, the fertility of man and beast, and the growth of crops. In this illustration he is depicted in destructive mood as the god of the storm, standing on a mountain range, brandishing a club in his right hand and holding a lance, perhaps representing forked lightning, in his left hand. His helmet has two horns, symbols of heroic power (p. 46), and his hair ends in two enormous curls. The small figure on the right standing on a pedestal may be a minor god.

It is perhaps not surprising that when the Israelites settled in Canaan and took up farming they were tempted to abandon Yahweh, the shepherd god, and to turn to the god who was responsible for the weather and the growth of crops.

Soon after the death of Joshua 'the Israelites did what was wrong in the eyes of the LORD, and worshipped the Baalim' (Judg. 2: 11; 'Baalim' is the plural form of 'Baal', and here means Canaanite deities). When Ahab, king of Israel, married Jezebel, a princess from Tyre in Phoenicia, a crisis arose, for the new queen brought to Ahab's court 'four hundred and fifty prophets of Baal' and 'four hundred prophets of the goddess Asherah' as her 'pensioners' (1 Kings 18: 19). Melkart was the name of the Phoenician Baal. The worship of the Baalim spread in Israel as a result, and it almost supplanted the worship of Yahweh. The struggle between the two forms of worship was fought out decisively on Mount Carmel (1 Kings 18: 17–40). This view (**174**) of the Mediterranean Sea and Haifa taken from the summit of Mount Carmel (map **1**) shows how impressive was the stage on which this drama was enacted.

174 *View from Mount Carmel*

175 *Shamash, the sun-god*

SUN WORSHIP

Idolatry was a temptation with which the Hebrews were frequently confronted and to which they sometimes fell. At times of serious religious decline in Israel the temple must have looked like a museum of pagan exhibits. There were 'objects made for Baal and Asherah', 'the symbol of Asherah' (footnote, 'sacred pole'), 'altars made by the kings of Judah . . . and the altars made by Manasseh', as well as 'all the host of heaven'; the symbols of sun, moon, and star worship (2 Kings 23: 4, 6, 12).

This stone relief (**175**) found at Sippar (map **4**) in 1881, and now in the British Museum, was probably carved in the middle of the ninth century B.C. It forms the upper part of a tablet recording the restoration by king Nabuaplaiddin of the sun temple at Sippar. Shamash, the sun-god, sits enthroned in a shrine on the right, and holds in his right hand a sceptre and a ring, the signs of his royal authority (p. 35). Before the shrine a large sun-disc rests on an altar which is suspended by ropes held by attendants on the roof of the shrine. Three worshippers, the king in the middle, stand in supplication before the altar.

Sun worship is strictly forbidden in the Law, but it must have been an attractive idea to the Hebrews. Israelites must not 'look up to the sun, the moon, and the stars . . . to bow down to them and worship them' (Deut. 4: 19), and the punishment for a man who falls into this error is emphatically stated: 'Stone him to death' (Deut. 17: 5). Josiah 'suppressed the heathen priests . . . as well as those who burnt sacrifices to Baal, to the sun and moon and planets and all the host of heaven' (2 Kings 23: 5), and he 'destroyed the horses that the kings of Judah had set up in honour of the sun at the entrance to the house of the LORD' (2 Kings 23: 11). A verse in Ezekiel suggests that sun worship was not completely eliminated in his day. He describes a curious ritual taking place in 'the inner court of the LORD's house' where 'some twenty-five men with their backs to the sanctuary and their faces to the east' were 'prostrating themselves to the rising sun' (Ezek. 8: 16).

THE TEMPLE

David planned to build a temple at Jerusalem, and he set aside money and materials for the purpose: 'a hundred thousand talents of gold and a million talents of silver, with great quantities of bronze and iron, more than can be weighed; timber and stone, too', according to 1 Chron. 22: 14, but numbers cannot always be taken seriously in descriptions of this kind in Chronicles. Solomon took seven years over the building of the temple, employing workmen from Tyre, in addition to 'a forced levy from the whole of Israel amounting to thirty thousand men' (1 Kings 5: 13).

The temple site was on a terrace to the north of the Royal Palace (map **56**), and the terrace enclosure can easily be identified in the aerial view of Jerusalem (**57**) by the domed building, known today as the Dome of the Rock, near its centre. The Dome of the Rock is a magnificent Muslim mosque, which was completed in A.D. 691. It covers a huge irregular outcrop of rock, which is the main feature inside the building (**176**). It is not known with certainty whether this rock served as the altar of Solomon's temple, or whether the inner shrine of the temple was built on it.

176 *The rock in the temple area, Jerusalem*

177 *Model of Solomon's temple, exterior*

No archaeological remains of Solomon's temple have ever been found, and we have no information about its appearance apart from the descriptions of it in the Bible. A model of the temple made under the direction of Professor P. L. Howland is on display at Agnes Scott College, Decatur, Georgia. It follows closely the specifications found in the books of Kings and Chronicles, and it is constructed to the scale of $\frac{3}{8}$ inch to a cubit. The external view of the model (**177**) shows the 'terrace . . . round both the sanctuary and the inner shrine' (1 Kings 6: 5); 'the two bronze pillars . . . , on the right side, . . . Jachin, . . . on the left side, . . . Boaz' (1 Kings 7: 15, 21); 'the bronze altar which stood before the LORD' (1 Kings 8: 64); and 'the Sea of cast metal . . . round in shape, . . . five cubits high, . . . mounted on twelve oxen, three facing north, three west, three south, and three east' (1 Kings 7: 23–5). 'The Sea was made for the priests to wash in' (2 Chron. 4: 6), 'the bronze altar' was for the sacrifices; 'the whole-offering, the grain-offering, and the fat portions of the shared-offerings' (1 Kings 8: 64), but the use of the two bronze pillars, if they had a use, is not known.

179 *Model of Solomon's temple, interior*

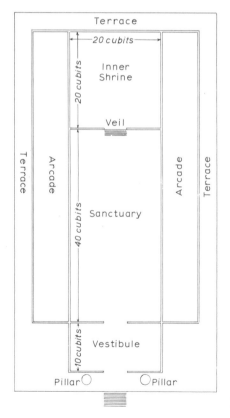

Terrace

20 cubits

Inner
Shrine

20 cubits

Veil

Terrace

Arcade

Arcade

Terrace

40 cubits

Sanctuary

10 cubits

Vestibule

Pillar ○   ○ Pillar

178 *Plan of Solomon's temple*

A plan of Solomon's temple can be drawn from the information given in the Bible (**178**), and the sectional view of the interior of Howland's model (**179**) conforms to this plan. In the model, the vestibule is on the right, the sanctuary is the large compartment in the middle, and the inner shrine is on the left. The sanctuary contains 'the golden altar and the golden table upon which was set the Bread of the Presence', and 'the lamp-stands of red gold, five on the right side and five on the left side' (1 Kings 7: 48f.). The inner shrine was a twenty-cubit cube in complete darkness. The model shows it containing 'two cherubim of wild olive, each ten cubits high' (1 Kings 6: 23), and 'the Ark of the Covenant of the LORD . . . beneath the wings of the cherubim' (1 Kings 8: 6). The inner shrine, also called 'the Most Holy Place', was 'partitioned off' from the sanctuary by 'a double door of wild olive' with 'a Veil with golden chains across in front of the inner shrine' (1 Kings 6: 16, 31, 21). The cherubim had the head of a man, the body of a lion, and the wings of an eagle, and they symbolized the presence of God.

Not all the temples built in about the tenth century B.C. had the same ground-plan as Solomon's (**178**). The foundations of temples excavated outside Palestine (for example, the royal chapel adjoining the palace at Tell Tainat in Syria, dated ninth century B.C.) conform to the plan of Solomon's temple, but the only Israelite temple of the period so far found in Palestine, that at Arad (map 1), shows an interesting variation. The temple at Arad was excavated by Yohanan Aharoni, and this diagram (**180**) shows a simplified plan of it. Three steps lead from the sanctuary (A) to a small inner shrine (B), and the two pillars are outside the sanctuary, not outside the porch as in Solomon's temple. There are two small altars in the inner shrine, one at either side of the entrance. A large courtyard (C) contains an altar (D) made of earth and small stones. The most interesting feature of this temple is the setting of the sanctuary (compare **178** and **180**). Aharoni thinks that the temple at Arad was built on an early Kenite hill-shrine which served as a central shrine for the whole region, and he puts forward the suggestion that the temples at Shiloh, Bethel, and Dan, and perhaps other places also, may have been built on the same plan as that at Arad.

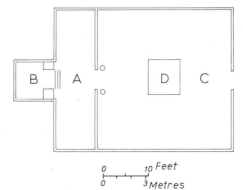

180 *Plan of the temple at Arad*

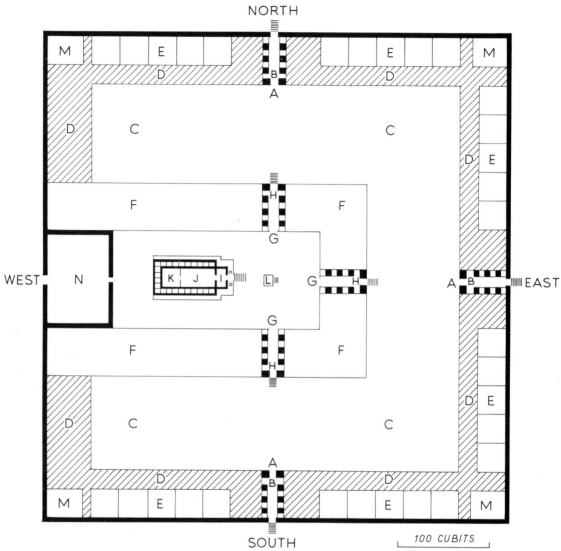

NORTH

WEST

EAST

SOUTH

100 CUBITS

181 *Plan of Ezekiel's temple*

EZEKIEL'S TEMPLE

Ezekiel describes the vision he saw of the temple to be built when the Jews returned to Palestine at the end of the exile in Babylon (Ezek. 40: 1–42: 20, 43: 13–17, 46: 19–24). The details in this description are not always clear, but an attempt has been made to draw a plan of this idealized temple (**181**). Solomon's temple was built on a low hill, Mount Zion, but Ezekiel's temple was to be built on top of 'a very high mountain' in a 'sacred area', a 500-cubit square surrounded by a wall six cubits high and six cubits thick. (The 'cubit' in this description of Ezekiel's temple is 'the long cubit which was one cubit and a hand's breadth'

(Ezek. 40: 5), probably about 56 centimetres or 22 inches.)

Seven steps lead to 'gateways' (A) on the north, east, and south sides of the sacred area, each gateway having three 'cells' on each side of it, and a 'vestibule' (B). These gateways are the entrances to the 'outer court' (C), which has a 'pavement' (D) round its edges with thirty rooms (E) built on it. The 'inner court' (F) is entered by three more gateways (G) similar to those leading to the outer court, except for the position of the vestibules (H). These gateways are approached by eight steps.

The temple itself stands in the inner court, and it has ten steps leading to its entrance. It consists of a 'vestibule' (I), a 'sanctuary' (J), and an 'inner shrine' (K), 'the Holy of Holies' (compare **178**). Like Solomon's temple, Ezekiel's temple stands on a 'raised platform' or 'terrace'. An altar (L) stands in the inner court. Its 'hearth' is 'twelve cubits long and twelve cubits wide, a perfect square'. In each corner of the sacred area are 'kitchens' (M) in which attendants 'boil the people's sacrifices', and to the west of the temple is a large building (N), the purpose of which is not stated. Other rooms for use in the ritual of temple worship are mentioned, but these would unduly complicate the plan and they are therefore not shown.

Ezekiel was shown 'the glory of the God of Israel coming from the east' and filling the temple. He was commanded to 'tell the Israelites about this temple, its appearance and proportions, that they may be ashamed of their iniquities', and to 'describe to them the temple and its fittings, its exits and entrances, all the details and particulars of its elevation and plan . . . so that they may keep them in mind and carry them out'. Ezekiel's dream never materialized, and there is no evidence to show that the restored temple in Jerusalem was anything more than a reconstruction of Solomon's temple.

JUDAISM

Judaism is the religion practised by orthodox Jews. Modern Judaism is the result of a long process of development in which each stage has contributed something of value. Perhaps the main development came when the temple was finally destroyed in A.D. 70. Judaism is based on the Law; Genesis to Deuteronomy, and the many additional laws that became necessary as each new situation arose. An orthodox Jew claims that the Law tells him what he ought to do from morning till night, from the cradle to the grave, and he strives to keep every detail of it scrupulously. The synagogue is the place where Jews worship on their sabbath day, Saturday, and on other important occasions, and where instruction in the Law is given.

182 *Bevis Marks Synagogue, London*

This photograph (**182**) of the Bevis Marks Synagogue, London, built in 1701, shows the essential features of a synagogue building: the raised platform from which the Law is read, at the bottom of the picture; the gallery, with a metal screen behind which the women and girls sit; and on the left the elaborately carved ark in which the scrolls of the Law are stored when not in use, surmounted by two tablets on which the ten commandments are written in Hebrew. The members of the congregation are waiting for a memorial service to begin and they are not wearing the tallit (p. 167) which is worn at the sabbath service.

Much care is lavished on the construction of the ark in a synagogue, and this picture (**183**) illustrates a modern ark in the Temple Emanuel, San Francisco. Made of bronze, with gold repoussé relief and rich jewel-coloured enamelling, it is the work of London artists and craftsmen. Note the star of David in the centre of the front panel and the symbols of the twelve tribes of Israel (pp. 57f.) in the corners of the panels.

183 *A modern ark*

184 *A scroll of the Law* **185** *Scrolls of the Law at Safad*

Scrolls of the Law are written by hand (**156**) on parchment skins fastened together to form a roll. The writing is in Hebrew and without vowels (pp. 138f.). The scrolls when not in use are covered with a mantle, and the handles are surmounted by decorations called finials. In this example (**184**) in the Jewish Museum, London, the mantle is beautifully embroidered, and the silver finials are finely shaped and have little bells hanging in them. These scrolls (**185**) seen inside the ark, are in a synagogue at Safad in Israel. The mantles are of richly embossed leather and the finials and bells are silver.

Silver breastplates are often hung on the scrolls when they are in the ark, perhaps in remembrance of the breastplate formerly worn by the high priest in the temple services. These silver breastplates (**186**) of the early nineteenth century are in the Mocatta Museum, University College, London.

186 *Silver breastplates*

187 *and* **188** *Prayer shawl and phylacteries*

REMINDERS OF THE LAW

A religion that lays special emphasis on the Law requires mnemonics to remind its adherents of the necessity of keeping the Law. Judaism has several. First, there is the tallit, or shawl, a scarf with tassels, which Jews wear when they pray. In these photographs a boy (**187**) and a man (**188**) are seen wearing striped prayer shawls over their shoulders. The eight strands of a tassel can be seen at the bottom of one of the pictures (**188**). The stripes have no religious significance. The rabbis reckon that the numerical value of the letters in the Hebrew word for tassels is 600, and that this added to the number of strands (8) and the number of knots in each tassel (5), gives a total of 613; and this, they say, is the number of items of instruction in the Law. Jews wear the tallit in obedience to the command which says, 'You must make tassels like flowers on the corners of your garments . . . Into this tassel you shall work a violet thread, and whenever you see this in the tassel, you shall remember all the LORD's commands and obey them' (Num. 15: 38f.).

Jews also wear phylacteries when they pray, one on the forehead and one on the hand and the arm, in obedience to the command which says, 'Bind them as a sign on the hand and wear them as a phylactery on the forehead' (Deut. 6: 8). In the first photograph (**187**) a boy is wearing the arm phylactery and is adjusting his head phylactery, and in the second photograph (**188**) the leather thong on the arm and the hand is very clearly seen. The thong must be wrapped round the arm

189 *Phylacteries*

seven times, and must make the Hebrew letter 'shin' (something like our letter W) on the hand. The leather boxes of the phylactery contain strips of parchment on which are written in Hebrew the essential portions of the Law: Exod. 13:1–10, 13:11–16, Deut. 6:4–9, 11:13–21. The leather thongs have been removed from this beautifully decorated pair of phylacteries (**189**), which are to be seen in the Jewish Museum, London.

The mezuzah is a third reminder of the obligation to keep the Law. This mezuzah (**190**) in the Jewish Museum, London, is made of ivory and is of the late fifteenth century. The central part of a mezuzah contains a small parchment roll on which is written in Hebrew, Deut. 6:4–9, 11:13–21. Mezuzahs are nailed on the door-posts of houses and rooms in which orthodox Jews live. The mezuzah is touched when passing through a doorway and the fingers that touched it are kissed as a reminder that the Law must be kept in the building or the room being entered. Speaking of the commands in the Law, the author of Deuteronomy says, 'Write them up on the door-posts of your houses and on your gates' (Deut. 6:9).

190 *An ivory mezuzah*

THE FESTIVALS

Judaism is a religion of many memorials, reminders of the great acts of God in Israel's history, and these memorials are enacted regularly in either solemn or joyous festivals, depending on the nature of the event being celebrated. The five rolls (p. 138) have since the sixth century A.D. been associated with the festivals: the Song of Songs with Passover, Ruth with the Feast of Weeks, Lamentations with the Ninth of Ab, Ecclesiastes with the Feast of Tabernacles, and Esther with Purim. Some of the festivals may have had an ancient agricultural origin, but they have been adapted to commemorate important events in Hebrew history.

The Passover or Feast of Unleavened Bread brings to mind the events of the exodus, especially the deliverance of Israel from the plague which smote Egypt when 'every first-born creature' died (Exod. 11: 5). Moses told the people to smear blood 'on the lintel and the two door-posts' of their houses. He said, 'The Lord . . . will pass over that door and will not let the destroyer enter your houses to strike you' (Exod. 12: 23). They were to tell their children, 'It is the LORD's Passover, for he passed over the houses of the Israelites in Egypt when he struck the Egyptians but spared our houses' (Exod. 12: 27). This engraving (**191**) shows a Jewish family of long ago eating the Passover meal. Note the roasted lamb bone, cakes of unleavened bread, the wine on the table, and the prayer books containing the Passover service being read by the people round the table. On the

191 *The Passover meal*

192 *The search for leaven*

193 *The Feast of Tabernacles*

evening before Passover begins, every trace of leaven (yeast) and leavened bread in the house must be searched out and burned. This engraving (**192**) shows the search for leaven in full swing. It is usually made into a jolly sort of game, and is much enjoyed by Jewish children.

The Feast of Ingathering celebrates the end of the fruit, oil, and wine harvest, but it is also kept as a reminder of the time when the Israelites encamped in the open air during the wilderness wanderings. This joyous festival is often called the Feast of Booths, or Tabernacles, because the Israelites were ordered to celebrate it by living in booths for seven days. The New English Bible uses 'arbours', and the instruction says, 'You shall live in arbours for seven days . . . so that your descendants may be reminded how I made the Israelites live in arbours when I brought them out of Egypt' (Lev. 23 : 42f.). This engraving (**193**) shows a family enjoying a meal in an arbour made by covering a wooden frame with branches and leaves, and decorating it with greenery and lanterns. This photograph (**194**) shows how a poor Jewish family today attempts to keep this festival by building a simple arbour over the doorway of their house.

194 *A booth*

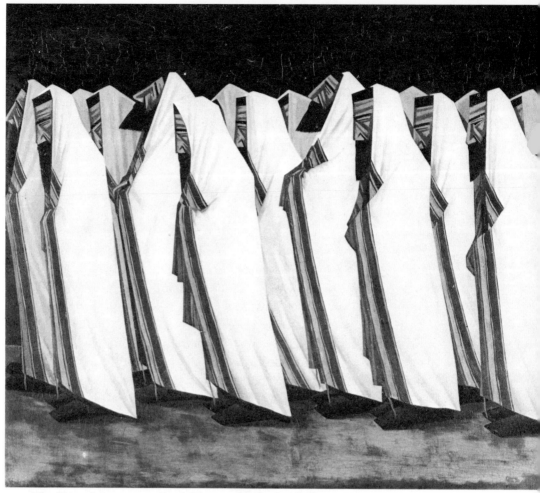

195 *The Day of Atonement, Jacob Kramer, Leeds Art Gallery*

The Day of Atonement is the most solemn of all the Jewish festivals, and this painting (**195**) by Jacob Kramer (1892–1962) in the City Art Gallery, Leeds, finely expresses the sense of sorrow associated with the occasion. Note the tallits worn by the priests, and tassels at the corners of them (p. 167). The accounts we have of the Day of Atonement are found in those parts of the Law that were written down after the exile, and it seems likely, therefore, that the ritual of the Day of Atonement was a consequence of the bitter experience of the Jews in exile in Babylon. Some elements of the ritual are probably much older than this, however: for example, the ceremony associated with the scapegoat.

The next painting (**196**), in the Lever Art Gallery, Port Sunlight, is the work of Holman Hunt (1827–1910). He is said to have spent two years in Palestine making sketches for his religious pictures, and to have encamped for some time on the shores of the Dead Sea to capture the sense of loneliness and tragedy he wished to convey in this picture. The reproduction here cannot bring out the gorgeous colouring of the sunset, which is a distinctive feature of the original work.

196 *The Scapegoat, Holman Hunt,*
Lever Art Gallery, Port Sunlight

On the Day of Atonement, the tenth day of the seventh month, the high priest took 'two he-goats' and cast lots to decide which goat was 'to be for the LORD', and which 'for the Precipice'. It was the latter that was 'driven away into the wilderness to the Precipice' as a scapegoat, bearing the sins of the people of Israel. The other goat was slaughtered as a sin-offering, and some of the blood was taken 'within the Veil' in the temple (**178**) and sprinkled 'on the cover and in front of it' (Lev. 16: 5–10, 15–17). Tradition says that the goat sent out into the wilderness had a garland of red wool tied between its horns, and that a similar piece of red wool was tied to the door of the sanctuary of the temple in Jerusalem. When the goat was pushed over the precipice, so the tradition continues, the red wool on the temple door turned to white, and the sins of the people were forgiven from that moment. Holman Hunt depicted the red wool on the scapegoat's head in his painting (**196**).

Two minor festivals, both joyous, are celebrated in addition to those mentioned above: Purim and Hanukkah. Purim recalls the story told in the book of Esther. This fresco (**197**) in the Chantilly Museum, France, by Filippino Lippi (1457–1504), depicts various incidents in the story. Esther is seen before king Ahasuerus,

197 *Esther and Ahasuerus, Filippino Lippi, Chantilly Museum, France*

198 *A scroll of Esther*

'the Ahasuerus who ruled from India to Ethiopia' (Esther 1 : 1), in competition with many other 'beautiful young virgins' (Esther 2 : 3), some of whom are parading before the king at the same time as Esther. Haman, the villain of the piece, plots 'to destroy all the Jews throughout the whole kingdom' (Esther 3 : 6), and lots are cast (*purim* is a Hebrew word which means 'lots') to discover the best day for the massacre to take place. The climax in the story comes when Esther discloses to the king, her husband, that she is a Jewess, and this turns the tables completely: the Jews are spared, and Haman is hanged on the gallows, 'seventy-five feet high', which he has prepared for Mordecai, his greatest enemy among the Jews (Esther 7 : 9f.). Haman's ten sons are also 'hung up on the gallows', and all the enemies of the Jews are destroyed, 'seventy-five thousand of those who hated them' (Esther 9 : 14, 16). Thereafter the Feast of Purim was to be kept as 'a holiday . . . , days of feasting and joy, days for sending presents of food to one another and gifts to the poor' (Esther 9 : 22). The festival is celebrated with enormous enthusiasm by Jews today, especially in Israel.

The entire book of Esther is read in the synagogue at two sessions during Purim, and the synagogue scroll of Esther is often richly decorated and a treasured possession. The illustrations at the beginning of this beautiful scroll (**198**) in the Jewish Museum, London, depict various incidents in the story. The top picture in the middle row shows Esther and the king enthroned, and the middle picture in the left hand column shows Haman and his ten sons hanging on an enormous gallows.

The other minor joyous festival is Hanukkah. It lasts eight days in remembrance of a legend told by the rabbis that one day's supply of oil burned for eight days and nights in the golden candelabra of the temple at Jerusalem, following the occasion when the priests chosen by Judas Maccabaeus 'purified the temple . . . and consecrated the temple courts' (1 Macc. 4 : 41–51) which had been defiled by Antiochus Epiphanes (p. 105).

This silver menorah (**199**) with eight containers for oil is the kind used in Jewish homes today for the celebration of Hanukkah. On the first night of the festival one lamp is lit, on the second night two, and so on, until the eighth night when all the lamps are lit together amid general rejoicing.

199 *A silver menorah*

200 *Blowing the shofar*

At the Jewish New Year, and on one or two other special occasions, the ram's horn, or shofar, is blown in the synagogue. The ceremony is illustrated here (**200**). Note the tallit worn by the priest. The shofar gives out a piercing, not very musical, note. To make a shofar, the horn is immersed in boiling water to soften it, shaped, and allowed to cool and harden again. It is usually engraved with a sharp needle whilst still hot, and a mouthpiece is often fitted at the narrow end of the horn.

The sabbath is considered by many Jews to be the most important festival of all. It is a weekly commemoration of the Creation; 'for in six days the LORD made the heavens and the earth, but on the seventh day he ceased work and refreshed himself' (Exod. 31: 17). It is also a reminder of the exodus from Egypt. The Law says, 'Remember that you were slaves in Egypt and the LORD your God brought you out with a strong hand and an outstretched arm, and for that reason the LORD your God commanded you to keep the sabbath day' (Deut. 5: 15). Jews welcome the sabbath at sunset on Fridays by lighting sabbath candles and drinking wine at a short religious ceremony called kiddush (the Hebrew word for 'sanctification'). This scene (**201**) is a common one on Friday evenings in the homes of orthodox Jewish families. On the sabbath day itself Jews attend services at the synagogue and rigidly abstain from doing any work, in obedience to the law which says, 'Keep the sabbath day holy . . . that day you shall not do any work, neither you, your son or your daughter, your slave or your slave-girl, your ox, your ass, or any of your cattle, nor the alien within your gates' (Deut. 5: 12–14).

201 *Kiddush on the eve of the sabbath*

BIBLIOGRAPHY

THE OLD TESTAMENT WORLD

AHARONI, Y. *The Land of the Bible: a Historical Geography*, Burns and Oates, 1967

BALY, D. *The Geography of the Bible*, Lutterworth, 1957

GROLLENBERG, L. H. *Atlas of the Bible*, Nelson, 1956

MAY, H. G. (ed.) *Oxford Bible Atlas*, Oxford University Press, 1962

NEGENMAN, J. H. *The New Atlas of the Bible*, Collins, 1969

BIBLICAL ARCHAEOLOGY

KENYON, K. M. *Archaeology in the Holy Land*, Benn, 1969

PFEIFFER, C. F. (ed.) *The Biblical World: a Dictionary of Biblical Archaeology*, Pickering and Inglis, 1964; Baker, Grand Rapids, 1966

THOMAS, D. W. (ed.) *Documents from Old Testament Times*, Nelson, 1958; Harper, 1965

WISEMAN, D. J. *Illustrations from Biblical Archaeology*, The Tyndale Press, 1963

WRIGHT, G. E. *Biblical Archaeology*, Duckworth, 1963

OLD TESTAMENT HISTORY

ANDERSON, B. *The Living World of the Old Testament*, Longmans, 1967

ACKROYD, P. R. *The People of the Old Testament*, Chatto and Windus, 1959

BRIGHT, J. *A History of Israel*, S.C.M. Press, 1960

New Clarendon Bible, vols 1–5, Clarendon Press

LIFE IN OLD TESTAMENT TIMES

HEATON, E. W. *Everyday Life in Old Testament Times*, Batsford, 1956

NOTH, M. *The Old Testament World*, A. and C. Black, 1966

VAUX, R. de *Ancient Israel: its Life and Institutions*, Darton, Longman and Todd, 1965

THE GROWTH OF THE OLD TESTAMENT

ANDERSON, G. W. *A Critical Introduction to the Old Testament*, Duckworth, 1959

KENYON, F. G. *The Story of the Bible*, John Murray, 1935

——*Our Bible and the Ancient Manuscripts*, Eyre and Spottiswoode, 1958

WESTERMANN, C. *Handbook to the Old Testament*, S.P.C.K., 1969; Augsburg, 1967

OLD TESTAMENT RELIGION

HERBERT, A. S. *Worship in Ancient Israel*, Lutterworth, 1959

ROWLEY, H. H. *The Faith of Israel*, S.C.M. Press, 1961

SCHOFIELD, J. N. *Introducing Old Testament Theology*, S.C.M. Press, 1964

SIMPSON, W. W. *Jewish Prayer and Worship*, S.C.M. Press, 1965. This book is mainly concerned with the later development of Judaism.

See also, companion with this volume, *Understanding the Old Testament* and *The Making of the Old Testament*, Cambridge, 1971.

INDEX OF TEXTS

Figures in italic type refer to pages